The
Quick
Reference
Guide to
Educational
Innovations

The Quick

Reference Guide to Educational Innovations

Practices,
Programs,
Policies,
and Philosophies

CAROLYN ORANGE

CORWIN PRESS, INC.
A Sage Publications Company
Thousand Oaks, California

For information:

Corwin Press, Inc.
A Sage Publications Company
2455 Teller Road
Thousand Oaks, California 91320
E-mail: order@corwinpress.com

Sage Publications Ltd.
6 Bonhill Street
London EC2A 4PU
United Kingdom

Sage Publications India Pvt. Ltd.
M-32 Market
Greater Kailash I
New Delhi 110 048 India

Printed in the United States of America

Library of Congress Cataloging-in-Publication Data

Orange, Carolyn.
    The quick reference guide to educational innovations: Practices, programs, policies, and philosophies / by Carolyn Orange.
        p. cm.
    Includes bibliographical reference and index.
        ISBN 0-7619-7815-1 (c) — ISBN 0-7619-7816-X (p)
        1. Educational innovations—Terminology. 2. Education—Experimental methods—Terminology. 3. Educational change—Terminology. 1. Title.
        LB1027 .069 2002
        370—dc21   2001008603

This book is printed on acid-free paper.

02   03   04   05   06   07   7   6   5   4   3   2   1

Acquisitions Editor: Rachel Livsey
Editorial Assistant: Phyllis Cappello
Typesetter/Designer: Hespenheide Design
Cover Designer: Tracy E. Miller
Indexer: Will Ragsdale

Contents

2 Programs 37

3 Policies 81

4 Philosophies, Theories, and Movements 95

Preface

"In education, change for good, change for better, and change for worse are inevitable and constant."

Education has been a target of reform for the past 100 years or so. The need for change in education has been a function of the changing needs of people and society. As history has moved from the Dark Ages to the Age of Enlightenment through the Age of Industry and on into the Information Age, changes in the needs of society have directed each of those moves. Enhancing the quality of the product of education—namely, our students—has been a critical motive for change through the years. Raising student test scores to be on a par with those of other countries has been a major incentive for the government's involvement with change in education. Improving the quality and standards of the teaching profession has also been a major motive for change. Collectively, these motives and incentives issue a call to action. Educators, reformers, theorists, businesspeople, practitioners, governments, parents, and administrators heard the call. They answered the call with a plethora of innovations: programs, models, theories, movements, practices, policies, legislation, mandates, and so on. The result is hundreds of educational innovations. Presented with so much to choose from, schools are like kids in a candy store, salivating over all the wonderful educational "candies" as they try to decide: Which ones do we choose? Which ones are the best? Which ones will have better outcomes? Which ones will raise test scores? Which ones are good for us?

Their dilemma reminds me of my dilemma as a child. When my mother received a box of chocolates for a special occasion, she would always make them available to everyone in the family. I had my favorite chocolates: nuts, caramel crunch, cherries, and others. My dilemma was that they were all covered with chocolate, so I did not know my favorite from my least favorite. How could I choose? I made a childish, egocentric decision to push my finger into the chocolate first, to test the center, with little thought to the waste that I was creating. Sometimes, I would bite the chocolate and throw the rest away if it was not one of my favorites. I could demolish a box of chocolates in short order. This went on for years. One day, after I had learned to read, I noticed that the sheet of paper that covered the chocolates identified the filling in each one. I had never noticed it before. But then again, I did not know to look for it. Sometimes it stayed in the box top. Most of the time, I was in such a hurry to get some chocolates that I paid no attention to the information available to me. My quest to find the right chocolate is analogous to schools trying to find the right remedy for the education ills that plague American campuses. Choosing, by trial and error, the best innovation for a particular educational setting or situation is the equivalent of sticking a finger in a chocolate to test the center rather than consulting the candy guide that clearly states what's in the chocolate. Choosing an appropriate innovation requires one to RATE (Research, Analyze, Test, and Evaluate) it first—or pay later, through wasted time and resources.

Although this reference book is not meant to be an exhaustive compilation, it does present a fairly comprehensive array of important innovations. My hope is that *The Quick Reference Guide to Educational Innovations* will inform the decision-making process, helping educational consumers cut through the "chocolate coating" of educational rhetoric and sales hype and go directly to the best innovation for them. I wish them bon appétit for the 21st century.

Acknowledgments

Very few accomplishments in life can be credited to only one person. . . . This book is no exception. Many people, named and unnamed, have contributed to the making of this book. I would like to acknowledge those whose impact has been most significant. First, I want to thank my graduate assistants—Rita Brewer, Sandra Whited, Carolyn Morgan, and Rebeca Kelly—for their tireless efforts and commitment to helping me finish this book. A very special thank-you to my editorial consultant and friend, Susan Dudley, New Jersey Writing expert. Many thanks to Anissa Pennick, Ruth Nelson, Claudia Brown, and Sandra Whited for their candid review of this book. A global thank-you to all the teachers and preservice teachers who gave input, but are too numerous to name. A special thank-you to our Dean, Blandina Cardenas, for her financial support and personal encouragement. I would like to acknowledge that a faculty Research Award, granted to me by the University of Texas at San Antonio, made it possible for me to complete this book in a timely fashion. I especially appreciate the expression of sympathy and encouragement from the UTSA faculty, from the parish of St. Philip's Episcopal Church, and from family and many friends, that made it possible for me to continue writing after the death of my father. A heartfelt thanks to Jay Whitney, former acquisitions editor of Corwin Press, who believed in me once again and championed my idea for this book. I am equally grateful to Rachel Livsey, Jay's successor, who picked up where he left off and carried the idea forward. I have reserved my last thank-you for my husband, Dr. John H. Orange, who always stands by me through the ups and downs, and the beginnings and the ends.

Introduction

We are knowledge gatherers by nature, sucking up knowledge from a variety of sources, storing what we have learned in our honeycombs of information. Once consumed, the nectar of knowledge becomes the honey of the mind, to be drawn on whenever we need to know or want to be in the know. We are such consummate consumers of knowledge because we feel woefully inadequate without it. We are uncomfortable in situations and settings where we lack understanding, awareness, or familiarity. We fear the humiliation of being uninformed, of being left out of conversations because we are ignorant of the topic. Lack of knowledge is a particularly important concern for those whose job it is to impart knowledge—namely, educators, administrators, parents, counselors, and others; they feel they are supposed to know something about most everything concerning education. It is difficult to keep abreast of all educational matters, because the number of educational innovations is increasing exponentially. A myriad of innovative practices, policies, programs, and philosophies have found their way into mainstream educational practice to join the legions of other bright ideas already in use.

A quick reference guide is needed because sorting through the muddle of educational innovations can be a daunting task. Educators, administrators, and others need information about educational innovations for comparative, informative, and evaluative purposes. We hear about innovations through the academic grapevine, where they become "buzzwords" making their way, on uninformed gossamer wings, through the educational network. Many of us frequently refer to these buzzwords and attempt to discuss them without adequate knowledge. The purpose of *The Quick Reference Guide to Educational Innovations* is to provide a useful tool and a ready reference for educators, helping them define, examine, and understand an array of educational innovations. Many preservice teachers are limited in their knowledge of practices, programs, policies, and philosophies. In fact, many practicing teachers and administrators find themselves at a disadvantage when asked to discuss current educational innovations. When considering both pre-service and veteran teachers for employment, school districts often attempt to assess their knowledge of current trends and innovations. School administrators and staff need to be wise consumers of reform and improvement programs. They must be able to sift through the educational rhetoric and marketing hype to get to the heart of an innovative offering. They must be able to compare the goals, benefits, and expected outcomes of a program or practice to make sure they are compatible with their needs. Parents are frequently at a loss when looking for the best school or instructional program for their child, because they are not familiar with cutting-edge innovation.

The Quick Reference Guide combines approximately 125 innovations in a single resource, providing explanations of their meanings, origins, contexts, and effectiveness. Readers familiar with the situations described above need no longer be at a disadvantage. This book should help them gain the knowledge to understand what is going on in the field of education and the savvy to stay abreast of new educational programs and innovations. It will help readers not only to make more informed decisions about the usefulness of certain innovations but also to ascertain the usefulness of current practices, policies, and procedures. This book is designed to serve a broad audience of practicing teachers, pre-service teachers, administrators, resource teachers, college professors, parents, and others who would like to stay abreast of new educational programs and innovations. Specific benefits for each group are as follows:

- Preservice and practicing teachers will become more aware of the array of practices, programs, policies, and so forth that are used in classrooms. They will become familiar with a variety of techniques and innovations for delivering instruction and addressing special needs. Teachers will gain a better will also be able to make informed decisions about the effectiveness of a variety of innovations.
- Administrators will have a reference tool to consult before implementing expensive, time-consuming projects, programs, or policies.
- College professors will find it easier to close the gap between theory and practice. They will be able to update their lectures to reflect the most current innovations.
- Parents and others concerned about issues in contemporary education will enhance their knowledge of instructional practices, programs, policies, and philosophies, and consequently enhance their involvement with the schools.

The high level of teacher input and feedback is a strength of this book. It is important for educational consumers to know what their peers think of the featured innovations. In the development phase of this book, approximately 35 practicing teachers brainstormed the initial list of innovations. In a later stage of development, the list of innovations was modified. Some topics were deleted and others were added. The decision to delete was based on the availability of research on the topic and on the scope of appeal.

Feedback on the programs in Section 2 of this guide was provided by respondents from a national panel of teachers who have earned distinction in education as Teachers of the Year. The Teachers of the Year who responded were from a variety of states including Montana, Hawaii, Idaho, Missouri, and Texas. They gave evaluative feedback on suggested applications, useful features, drawbacks, and limitations of the programs. I surveyed these teachers by email; each respondent was paid a consultant's fee for completing the survey. In the final stage of editing the book, several exemplary teachers were invited to review the content, suggest changes, point out errors and omissions, and evaluate the book's overall usefulness and quality. Those surveyed said that *The Quick Reference Guide* would be a useful addition to anyone's educational library. Although it is primarily intended to be a reference text, it is also recommended as a supplemental text, or for the following types of courses:

- Teacher preparation
- Professional development
- Learning theories
- History of American education
- Educational methods and approaches
- Educational psychology
- Educational innovations
- Special education
- Educational leadership

The Quick Reference Guide to Educational Innovations is more comprehensive than most books of its kind. Similar books on the market usually focus only on practices or programs, and the number of entries is often limited. The scope of this guide is another strength. As mentioned earlier, it addresses approximately 125 educational innovations that are practices, programs, policies, philosophies, or movements. The primary objectives of the entries are to instruct, educate, and illuminate. This book does not seek to promote or discredit any innovation, although teachers' opinions and my reflections may inadvertently do so.

The book groups the innovations into four sections or categories— Practices; Programs; Policies; and Theories, Philosophies, and Movements. Innovations are organized alphabetically within each section. Section 1, "Practices," features an example of each entry. The Teacher of the Year comments and my reflections are offered in Section 2, "Programs." My reflections are based on my teaching experience, literature, graduate student input, current research, and media coverage for each topic. Section 3, "Policies," offers a description of current policies; some—such as zero tolerance—are controversial. Section 4, "Theories, Philosophies and Movements," features short essays on important theories, psychological schools of thought, and educational trends and movements. Current topics, such as situated learning and constructivism, are discussed. An educational cartoon introduces each section and reflects its content. References are provided for further research on any topic. Reading this book should help to quiet the drone of buzzwords that gives a false impression of knowledge, replacing it with the quiet confidence of being informed.

About the Author

Carolyn Orange, PhD, is Associate Professor of Educational Psychology at the University of Texas at San Antonio. She teaches Psychological Basis of Learning, Learning and Development of the School-Age Child, Human Growth and Development, and Psychology of Human Motivation. She has PhD and master's degrees in Educational Psychology from Washington University and a bachelor's degree from Harris Stowe State College. She began her teaching career in the St. Louis Public Schools, where she taught for a number of years. Her work as an educator has spanned about 25 years, including some time working for two corporations. She has worked as a teacher, substitute teacher, consultant, researcher, and professor in a variety of educational settings: elementary, secondary, English as a second language (ESL), Montessori, special education, adult education, art, and higher education.

Dr. Orange has produced a video on self-regulation and has developed a Self-Regulation Inventory that is currently being used in Italy. She has published articles in journals such as the *Journal of Adolescent and Adult Literacy, Journal of Experimental Education, Roeper Review, Journal of Communications and Minority Issues, Journal of Black Studies, NASSP: Curriculum Report,* and *High School Journal.* In 2001, she was appointed to the review board of the *Journal of Communications and Minority Issues.* She was included in *Who's Who Among American Teachers* for 1996, 1998, and 2000, and in the 2001 edition of *Who's Who in America.* Dr. Orange's current research interests are envirosocial factors affecting student achievement. She is the author of the bestseller, *25 Biggest Mistakes Teachers Make and How to Avoid Them.*

This book is dedicated to my late father, Mr. William Montgomery Sr., who passed from this life as I was writing this book. He came into this world a brilliant man, but his spark was never attended to, nurtured, or encouraged to grow. His was a light of promise, often diminished by hardships but never fully recognized or appreciated. Few saw this light, and none will ever see it again. But Daddy, I saw it—it enlightened me and it will forever shine through me and hopefully through my children and theirs, fulfilling the promise of the eternal light that yours was meant to be.

1

Practices

*An educational practice is a customary
action in performing or teaching an academic task.*

© 1996 Randy Glasbergen.

GLASBERGEN

"I couldn't do my literacy homework because
my computer has a virus and so do all
my pencils and pens."

Advance Organizer

A controversial aspect of Ausubel's learning theory (1963) suggests a strategy of providing, in advance of a lesson, an introductory statement that is abstract or broad enough to encompass all of the information or material that will follow. Organizers facilitate the connection of new information to what the learner already knows. This strategy provides the "big picture," thereby conceptually bridging the gap between what is known and what is to be learned. Graphic organizers, or spatial displays of text, metaphors, models, diagrams, and analogies can be effective organizers (Mayer, 1983; Banikowski & Mehring, 1999; Robinson & Kiewra, 1995).

Ex: Table 1.1 is a graphic organizer for teaching categories of advance organizers.

Table 1.1   Types of Advance Organizers

Types of Advance Organizers	Function	Example
Comparative	Activate existing knowledge	Verbal cues
Expository	Provide prerequisite knowledge	Definition(s)

Applied Learning

Applied learning, as the term suggests, is a strategy for making practical application of what is learned by integrating subject matter with authentic learning experiences. Learners are given tasks that not only test their skills and knowledge but also require higher-order thinking skills. Curriculum and instruction integrate these tasks. Students effectively learn the skills and knowledge presented in the subject matter. School districts develop individual applied learning standards for their district.

Ex: Performance standards for designing a product for a specific purpose may involve skills such as:

1. Generating ideas for a design
2. Representing the problem
3. Devising a plan
4. Implementing the plan
5. Evaluating the finished product using teacher-provided success criteria

Art Galleries

Traditionally, art galleries were public buildings used to exhibit large collections of art, or private galleries that featured one or two artists. They are a good source of information for field trips and art classes. Today, this concept has been extended to include student galleries, online galleries, and electronic galleries. Student galleries are used to showcase students' artwork and may be an essential part of art therapy. Online galleries feature images of artwork, digitized and captured for 24-hour viewing. Electronic galleries host a variety of works in various media. They are interactive in that they invite submissions from all over the world. Students are encouraged to submit their work and critique the works of others.

Ex: Eastern Washington University has an electronic gallery on the Internet. It is available at http://visual.arts.ewu.edu.

Art Therapy

Art therapy is a form of psychotherapy that helps children express their emotions using simple art materials. Children may have difficulty articulating emotionally painful experiences. Art therapy helps them to break through the barriers of self-expression to lay a foundation for healing through nonverbal means. This form of therapy is relatively safe. It offers children an opportunity to explore painful thoughts and feelings in a nonthreatening environment. Art therapy employs a variety of art media such as paint, clay, sculpture, collage, and masks to encourage graphic representation of thoughts and feelings (American Art Therapy Association, 1999).

Ex: Creating masks can be an effective medium for people to hide the true self. Behind a mask, they may be more willing to open up and share their true feelings and thoughts. Wearing a mask can be an effective venue for unlocking inhibitions and for revealing secret selves.

Assertive Discipline

Assertive discipline is a widely used, highly controversial method of classroom management that is based on a firm set of rules, penalties, and rewards. Marlene and Lee Canter (1992) developed a discipline model based on hundreds of observations of successful teachers. The Canter model proposes that when students are corrected or reprimanded, the teacher should communicate the problem or misbehavior and follow up by stating the expected behavior. After clearly stating their expectations, teachers should be assertive and consistently apply negative consequences when expectations are not met. They should apply positive consequences when expectations are met. Assertive discipline is based on the premise that teachers should try to catch students in the act of being good and let students know when they like what the students are doing. Although teachers have the right to expect and demand responsible behavior from students, they do not have the right to embarrass, ridicule, or humiliate their students The model advocates praise first and punishment as a last resort. The Canter carrot-on-the-stick, crack-the-whip philosophy is not without its critics. Opponents believe that assertive discipline may have long-term negative effects on children's attitudes toward school (Long, 1991). Some critics are concerned that students will behave appropriately only for reward, or from fear of punishment, and not because it's the right thing to do. Teacher behavior is critical to the success of this model; they are expected to be assertive rather than hostile or passive.

Ex: A student interrupts while the teacher is teaching a concept. An assertive response would be, "We don't interrupt someone when they're talking. Hold your question until I finish speaking, and I'll be happy to answer your question at that time." Hostile response: "Sit down and shut your big mouth." A passive response might be, "Please let me finish what I was saying." The assertive response states the problem and follows up with the expected behavior.

Authentic Assessment

Authentic assessment is a reality-based form of evaluation designed to gather information about students. An important characteristic of authentic assessment is that it attempts to assess students in the context of situations that parallel or approximate the real world. Authentic assessment is sometimes referred to as performance assessment. To be effective, authentic assessment should incorporate some form of self-assessment that requires realistic student involvement in the evaluation of their performance and achievement.

Authentic assessment offers an alternative to using traditional assessment such as standardized tests for young children. The appropriateness and validity of using standardized group tests for primary students are questionable. The highly verbal, abstract nature of standardized tests and the young age of the test takers confounds the interpretation of student scores. This is particularly true for low scores, where it's difficult to know whether young students found the content difficult or the instructions confusing. To be effective, it is imperative that authentic assessment be instructionally and developmentally appropriate (Pett, 1990). A drawback of using authentic assessment is that it requires a lot of time. Rubric assessment on the computer is a more efficient, effective method. The rubric or scoring guide can be quickly set up and easily revised or reused.

Ex: Portfolios are an example of authentic assessment. Students and teachers can assemble samples of students' work for review to determine student progress.

Behavior Management Centers

The Behavior Management Center (BMC) is a schoolwide discipline plan designed to maintain a safe, orderly school environment. All behavioral problems are addressed in a central location, staffed with a trained paraprofessional working in consultation with school counselors, administrators, and other relevant personnel. The school establishes schoolwide rules and standards that are developmentally appropriate for the various grade levels. Uniform standards ensure fairness and consistency in the application of consequences. The schoolwide plan provides maximum opportunity for students to learn by maximizing engagement. Teachers can spend maximum time on instruction once freed from the distraction and disruption of discipline. Prevention is a major strategy. Schoolwide rules and standards are taught and reinforced at every opportunity. Children who fail to comply with the schoolwide standards are referred to the center, and their parents are notified after repeated warnings and time-outs.

Violations include but are not limited to discourtesy, defiance, and disturbing or disrupting behaviors. The principal should immediately address severe or extreme behavior. Upon entering the center, the children are usually given a 10- to 15-minute reflective period, during which they are instructed to think about the behavior or problems that occurred in the classroom. The children may remain in the center for 15 to 30 minutes, depending on grade level. During that time, they are expected to do their class work. If children have too many visits to the center within a short period of time, it is reasonable to suspect that the center may be functioning as a negative reinforcer for them (Skinner, 1953), and that developing a classroom plan may be more appropriate. If removal from class, in-school suspension, and intervention fail, the school may resort to more comprehensive measures involving the principal, counselor, and parents. Meanwhile, the teacher is still allowed to focus more on instruction and maintain an orderly classroom.

Ex: A discussion of the structuring of the Lettie Marshall Dent Elementary School Behavior Management Center is available online at http://www.smcps.k12.md.us/des/des-bmc.htm.

Behavioral Objectives

Behavioral objectives are desired instructional outcomes expressed in terms of observable behaviors. The purpose of behavioral objectives is to communicate to students what is expected, under what conditions, and how the results will be assessed. Behavioral objectives encourage teachers to be precise about what they expect to achieve and help them develop a means of assessing the outcomes. Mager (1975) developed a three-part system for writing instructional objectives:

- Behavior—what the student will do
- Conditions—under what givens or conditions they will do it
- Criteria or mastery level—how well the student must do

Gronlund (1995) advocates a different approach. He prefers stating a general objective and then giving specific examples of sample behaviors.

Ex: A Mager-type objective might read as follows: (a) Behavior: A student will learn to multiply fractions; (b) Condition: of the type $1/2$, $1/3$; and (c) Criteria or mastery level: must get 8 out of 10 correct.

Benchmarks

The concept of benchmarks is borrowed from the profession of surveying, in which the term *benchmark* refers to a point of reference. In education, benchmarks are a form of measurement by specific standards. Standards are descriptions of key tasks that students are expected to perform at various grade levels. They are the foundation of standards-based education and assessment. Benchmarks indicate what should be taught and provide established standards for student performance.

Benchmarks may be written for intervals of grade levels, for each grade level, or as a course description. Course descriptions are more appropriate for high school.

Benchmarks articulate a clear hierarchy of knowledge and skills required at a particular grade level, based on what experts have determined a student should know at that level. Traditional multiple-choice tests or performance tasks based on real-world scenarios may be used to effectively assess benchmarks. Both approaches have drawbacks; traditional tests do not require students to apply knowledge, and performance-based tests are too time consuming.

Ex: A 600-page, internationally acclaimed compendium of standards and benchmarks for K–12 education is being developed by the McREL (Mid-Continent Research for Education and Learning) Institute (Kendall & Marzano, 2000) and is available online.

Bibliotherapy

Bibliotherapy is a means of helping people solve problems through the use of books. This idea of promoting healing through books is particularly useful for working with children. Influenced by the developmental limitation known as animism, young children readily attribute lifelike characteristics to inanimate objects such as characters in a book. These children have the perfect mindset for this type of therapy. Bibliotherapeutic intervention is a deliberate course of action that demands careful planning. Topics such as divorce, fears, substance abuse, adoption, and other similar topics are suitable for bibliotherapy. However, counselors and teachers should be careful not to cross children's personal boundaries or violate their trust and confidence when using this technique.

Ex: *Sometimes My Mom Drinks Too Much*, the children's book by Kevin Kenny and Helen Krull, may be used as bibliotherapy for young children faced with the trauma of living with an alcoholic parent. Seeing another child in a similar situation may give them some comfort, by letting them know they are not alone.

Block Scheduling

Block scheduling is an innovative approach to scheduling courses that has not only gained popularity but also attracted criticism. Criticisms of block scheduling are that the schedules can be confusing, some classes are not suited for block scheduling, and seeing students every other day makes teaching more difficult. Some positive observations about block scheduling are that teachers are better able to meet the needs of individual students, to offer smaller classes, and to provide more in-depth study. It is easier to offer remedial classes with block scheduling. In some situations, students can fail a subject and not be held back a year because there is time to make it up.

Ex: Here are four types of scheduling models:

- 4 x 4 Block model—Two semesters of four classes, each 90 minutes long. If warranted, additional time may be added for remediation.
- A/B schedule—Students go to periods 1 through 4 on A days and 5 through 8 on B days. Subjects may be studied over the school year rather than the semester.
- Microcourses—Courses of very short duration are usually paired with traditional courses. Microcourses are useful for extending these classes for longer periods of time.
- Modified trimester—This is an example of using a current schedule and modifying where necessary to accommodate areas such as remediation, advisory, and enrichment.

Brainstorming

Brainstorming is a technique for generating ideas. In a brainstorming session, several people get together and rapidly come up with ideas without stopping to evaluate them. The underlying premise is that participants will be less inhibited and more likely to generate good ideas if they don't feel that their ideas will be rejected. Allowing several minutes of quiet before the session begins has been especially effective for some groups.

Ex: The organization known as Teen Think Tanks of America offers an added dimension to brainstorming as their members engage in discussions about ways to solve the problem of school violence. The teenagers conduct brainstorming sessions on personal computers using electronic meeting software developed by Groupsystems.com of Tucson, Arizona. They generate hundreds of ideas and select the best. The Teen Think Tanks Web site is at http://rod1.com/teens/ttta01c.htm.

Career Days

Career days are special days devoted to exposing students to a variety of careers. Schools invite various companies to set up tables or booths in a facility on or off the school campus. Company representatives discuss their occupations and the skills and knowledge students will need to pursue the same type of work. Representatives may also have information about internships, summer jobs, part-time employment, and the process for securing full-time employment. Students may browse freely, visiting companies and careers that attract them, or they may move from table to table at pre-determined intervals. Some of these programs have been criticized for channeling minority and immigrant children to low-level, labor, or service-intensive careers. For career days to be effective, all students should receive maximum exposure to their choice of all of the careers represented at the event. As much as possible, the ethnic makeup of the representatives should reflect the diversity of the student body.

Ex: An innovative approach to career days is called virtual job shadow (http://jobshadow.monster.com). Students across the country can shadow participating career mentors on the Internet, learning about the education and skills needed for a variety of jobs. This project is part of the national Groundhog Job Shadow Day, which gives students a chance to experience the world of work firsthand. Not all students are able to go into a workplace. Fortunately, students who cannot physically go into a workplace can do so using their computer or school computers. The project starts every February 2 and continues through the end of the month.

Classwide Peer Tutoring

Classwide Peer Tutoring (CWPT) is an instructional technique based on research developed by Juniper Gardens Children's Project in Kansas City, Kansas, in collaboration with a group of classroom teachers (Delquadri, Greenwood, Stretton, & Hall, 1983). This strategy uses peer-mediated instruction to improve instruction for students with and without learning disabilities. However, it does primarily target students who have difficulty learning. It is designed to help these students acquire and retain basic skills. Students work in dyads as either the tutor or the tutee. Tutoring is usually conducted in pairs, classwide. Students reverse roles frequently throughout the process. Participants need two training sessions of about 30–45 minutes each to learn tutoring procedures. The actual peer tutoring is conducted in a competitive game format, in which the tutor follows CWPT tutoring procedures. The tutor covers the assigned material, corrects errors using an answer sheet; awards points for correct responses, and provides feedback for responses. Tutors cover as much material as possible in the allocated 10-minute time frame. Each team earns points based on the number of items correctly completed.

During the classwide peer session, the teacher functions as a facilitator, walking around, monitoring the process, and awarding points for appropriate tutoring behaviors. Students rotate the tutor role, completing as many items as possible in the 30-minute session.

Ex: Reddy and others (2000) used Classwide Peer Tutoring to teach health and safety topics to mildly retarded students. Students received tutoring on drugs, poisons, body functions, potential dangers, and how to prevent accidents. Using CWPT, students increased their knowledge of these subjects significantly.

Collaborative Learning

Collaborative learning is an instructional method that encourages students of varying levels of achievement to help each other succeed. Students work in groups to master material presented by the teacher. Collaborative learning is based on the premise that learning is essentially social, and it is fostered through communication. Students listen, argue, discuss, explain, and teach in their efforts to help each other master the academic content presented by the instructor. Group members are responsible for making sure all members understand the material.

Ex: A common form of collaborative learning is student team learning. Here are some popular types:

- Student Teams-Achievement Divisions (STAD)—Students work in groups of four or five to ensure that everyone comprehends the material, but they are evaluated individually. STAD is used in grades 2–12 in all subjects and in colleges across all disciplines.
- Teams-Games Tournaments (TGT)—TGT is like STAD except that students are evaluated as a group.
- Jigsaw II—This method is used in grades 3–12 and at the college level, where students compete in academic tournaments. Groups are evaluated both individually and as a group.

Communities in Schools

Communities in Schools (CIS) is a nationwide, independent network of 154 local and 15 state CIS offices that serve 1,500 school sites. The sole mission of Communities in Schools is to build a bond between schools and communities by connecting community resources with young people who need these resources to stay in school, to learn, and to prepare for life. CIS operations offer students a hands-on, high-tech experience and the opportunity to work with caring adults in an atmosphere of caring and concern for children. CIS provides students with a community of tutors, counselors, and health care workers. Community champions act as advocates for children, rallying support services for them. CIS founder and President Bill Milliken insists that CIS is not a program; it is a needed connection or relationship builder for schools and communities.

Ex: Communities in Schools in Texas provides school-based social services and links to community resources to help young people.

Computer-Assisted Instruction

Computer-assisted instruction (CAI) primarily refers to using computers to supplement traditional instruction. Common practices are using computers for drill and practice, for simulations, and as tutorials. CAI is often used interchangeably with computer-based instruction (CBI). The difference between computer-assisted instruction and computer-based instruction is that CBI is a broader term that refers to almost any form of computer use in the classroom. It goes beyond drill and practice, tutorials, and simulations to include word processing, programming, doing research on the Internet, developing databases, constructing Web sites, and similar activities. Research has shown that using CAI to supplement traditional instruction has achieved results that are superior to using instruction alone.

Ex: Popular uses of CAI are computer simulation games, like "Sim City" and "Where in the World Is Carmen Sandiego," that help students improve their social studies, writing, and reference skills.

Concept Mapping

Concept maps are hierarchical representations of concepts and relationships or links to other concepts in graphical form. There are a wide variety of approaches for implementing concept maps and many variations such as semantic webs, mind maps, flowcharts, and hierarchies. Teachers or students may construct concept maps. The maps are constructed by identifying links among concepts, stating or showing how they are related, and refining those relationships to produce a visual hierarchical representation of subordinate and superordinate concepts. Concept mapping improves understanding for both teachers and students. It helps teachers to understand what they're trying to teach and to determine if students are learning what they're intended to learn.

Ex: Figure 1.1 is a concept map illustrating the technique of concept mapping.

Figure 1.1 A Partial Concept Map of Concept Mapping

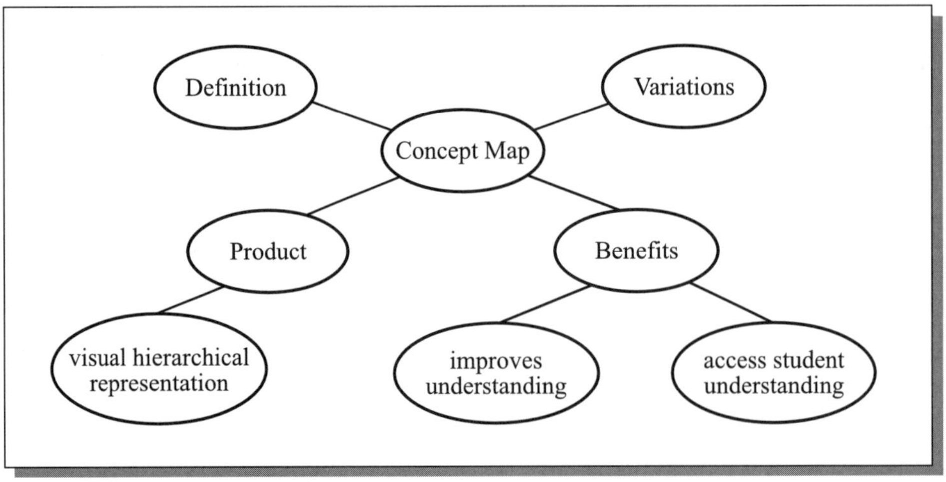

Conflict Resolution

Conflict resolution is an attempt to solve problems, heal relationships, or promote peaceable solutions to contentious situations. Mediation is an effective method that employs a neutral third party to help those in dispute find a peaceful, mutually acceptable solution to their problem.

Ex: Peer mediation is used in schools to help students resolve conflict. Designated students are trained to mediate conflict between disputing parties. Any party to the dispute can request mediation.

Content Mastery

Content mastery is a service that provides individual instruction to special education students outside the regular classroom. All required instruction is done in the classroom. Supplemental instruction is provided in a "content mastery center" for students with mild disabilities or students needing extra help. These centers are highly specialized resource centers, usually staffed by a trained professional and/or a full-time assistant. The content mastery staff collaborates with the classroom teacher to ascertain and serve students' needs. The concept of content mastery may vary across school districts.

Ex: A content mastery center that offers a variety of enrichment materials may be set up in a school media library or in an individual classroom.

Cooperative Learning

Cooperative learning is a method of student team learning in which students of varying levels of performance are grouped together and share responsibility for each other's performance and achievement. The cooperative learning group is typically composed of four students: a high-achieving student, two with low ability, and one with low achievement. The design places a lot of responsibility on the achieving student, who is more likely to know whether the other students are mastering the content. Effectively, the achieving child may become a teacher of sorts, because he or she has a better command of how to learn. This design has been found to be very useful for some classrooms, particularly when the goal is just to transmit some basic knowledge. It could be more difficult to use if students had to employ higher-level thinking strategies.

The premise of cooperative learning is that discussing ideas with others sharpens one's own understanding. Cooperative learning methods, with students working in small groups to help each other learn, are considered the most widely accepted, effective teaching methods.

Ex: Cooperative learning also uses the student-team learning techniques (see "Collaborative Learning") that were developed at Johns Hopkins University. These techniques suggest that when students are evaluated as a group, they have more incentive to ensure that the entire group achieves. The following forms of student-team learning are primarily used at the elementary level:

- Team Accelerated Instruction–Mathematics (TAI)—This technique, used for grades 3–6, combines individual instruction with cooperative learning.
- Cooperative Integrated Reading Composition (CIRC)—This is a comprehensive approach to reading instruction where students work in reading groups and in cooperative learning groups.

Core Knowledge

Core knowledge is an idea of a fair, success-oriented model curriculum for all children. It is a product of the research conducted by the Core Knowledge Foundation. The goal of core knowledge is to provide students with a solid, shared, and specific core curriculum to foster strong foundations of knowledge at each grade level (Core Knowledge Foundation, 1999). A basic principle is that a defined body of knowledge should form the core of a curriculum from preschool to kindergarten. This knowledge should be clearly defined, very specific, and properly sequenced to ensure fairness for all children. The intent is that knowledge will build on prior knowledge each year. Each child will be taught a shared body of knowledge used in our culture—a knowledge that is frequently used by writers and speakers, and that almost everyone should know (Core Knowledge Foundation, 1999). This body of knowledge attempts to answer the question of what children need to know in math, science, history, geography, and language arts. The sequence was determined by research and expert input provided by scientists, parents, teachers, and other professional groups affiliated with the Core Knowledge Foundation. There is a growing network of Core Knowledge schools across the United States.

Ex: An example of a science strand would be to teach basic information about magnets in early grades, adding new information at each grade level until students are studying electromagnets or something more complex.

Detention

Detention or forced, punitive delay has become a popular alternative to corporal punishment and suspension. The practice is somewhat penal in that students are detained when they would normally be free—during recess, on Saturdays, before and after school, or in study halls. In most cases, students are deprived of any social contact. Therein lies the power of detention; the threat of missing fun, activities, and contact with friends can be a potent deterrent. To be effective, detention should be for a reasonable period of time. Imposing excessive time periods may spawn a whole new set of problems. Offenses that qualify for detention should be clearly articulated and communicated to the student. The response to these offenses should be appropriate and equitable. Racial and gender bias cannot be tolerated. Detention is most likely to be inefficient if students are not engaged in meaningful work and are allowed to socialize. Giving students the freedom to interact freely with other students may inadvertently reward students for misbehavior or noncompliance. Frequent trips to detention provide evidence of its ineffectiveness for the students involved. In fact, in such cases detention may be more of a negative reinforcer than a deterrent. Detention should be supervised by caring, qualified personnel rather than security guards or the like, which may soften the penal persona that seems an integral part of detention.

Ex: A new concept in detention is being offered to chronically truant high school students, who are encouraged to express their aggression through percussion—beating drums to earn detention points. Considering students enjoy it and try not to miss it, I am not sure if the drums class shares the same premise as detention; but it does use a more positive approach to achieve the same goal of changing student behavior.

Direct Instruction

Direct Instruction (DI) is short for DISTAR, or Direct Instruction System for Teaching Arithmetic and Reading. Direct instruction is a scripted, phonics-based reading program in which teachers operate from detailed scripts to tell children what they need to know. This method is reminiscent of the back-to-basics type of instruction that is very highly controlled by the teacher. Some see it as authoritarian. Direct instruction arrived on the scene in about 1968 and writhed around in controversy until the early seventies, when interest in this type of instruction began to wane. The original theory of DI, opposed by Sigfried Englemann and colleagues in 1964, was conceptually behaviorist. It proposed that the effectiveness of a teaching strategy can be measured by change—or by no change—in behavior. If a child failed, the problem was not cognitive; rather, something was wrong with the organization or presentation of the material. Direct Instruction is enjoying renewed popularity as students in DI schools make impressive gains in their math and reading scores.

Ex: Robert Slavin's Model of Direct Instruction (Slavin, 1997) recommends telling students what they will be learning, and to make sure they have the necessary skills for the lesson. After presenting the new information, teachers should ask relevant questions to make sure that students understand. Students should be given opportunities to reflect on the information and to practice new skills. Typically, teachers review students' work and give them feedback. Sometimes students are allowed to practice at home, or they are given specific follow-up assignments as homework.

Discovery Learning

Discovery learning is an instructional method rooted in Gestalt psychology. It encourages learners to be intuitive and find out for themselves by drawing on prior knowledge and experience. This practice dates back to John Dewey (1938) and his theory of hands-on learning in the laboratory school, and to Jerome Bruner (1967) and his disciplined inquiry theory of categorization. The idea is that if learners are presented with an interesting learning challenge, they may experience some cognitive disequilibrium, which may in turn compel them to find out more about the problem in order to restore their balance or equilibrium. The teacher assumes the role of facilitator in this finding-out process. Although the level of teacher participation may vary, discovery learning is more effective with less teacher intervention and control. In fact, the learner functions as a constructionist, organizing and constructing knowledge in a meaningful way to make sense of the information.

A major limitation of discovery learning is that it may require a lot of time, and there is no guarantee that the student will eventually make sense of the learning challenge. Despite its limitations, I believe discovery learning is very effective. Students gain more ownership using this method; constructing knowledge makes it more meaningful and facilitates retention. This type of learning can be satisfying, and if successful, can serve as an impetus for further success. Discovery learning has moved away from the concept learning of Bruner (1967) to what is referred to as scientific discovery learning (DeJong & Van Joolingen, 1998).

Ex: In high school, my daughter's class was assigned a project in which students were required to design a mousetrap car. Students arrived in class to find tables filled with foam cups, rubber bands, small wheels, tongue depressors, and so forth. They did not know what to make of it, which caused some disequilibrium. The teachers' expectations were that the cars would run, and students were graded according to how many inches their car traveled. Although she was frustrated initially, my daughter did some research, and through trial and error eventually designed a car that traveled several inches.

Distance Learning

Distance learning is instruction delivered by a teacher to students at a remote site, via a camera that is strategically placed in a room. The teacher and students can see each other as they engage in an interactive dialogue. The teacher can control most aspects of the exchange. A camera at the podium digitizes and projects documents, notes, transparencies, pictures, and so forth. The teacher can write on the blackboard or on paper at the camera station. Typically, some students are at the teacher's site, and their counterparts are beamed in from a remote site. In this setting, students can interact with each other and hear each other's questions. Distance learning classrooms must be designed to meet certain specifications. They can be very expensive.

Distance learning is a popular concept in colleges and universities because students can be in different locations and still register for classes. This allows universities to increase enrollment beyond the capacity of their physical plant. Faculty can virtually be in two or more places or campuses at once. The university is not limited to recruiting students in the immediate area. Criticisms of this method of instruction are that it is impersonal, boring, and frustrating when technical problems occur. Distance learning is most effective when students and teachers are comfortable with current technology. Distance learning is at the heart of the concept of the virtual university.

Education Portals

Education portals are used to provide a more secure, protected environment for students accessing the Internet. These portals collect and organize relevant Web data and resources, filtering and eliminating material unsuitable for young students (Lindroth, 2000). Education portals are useful for planning lessons, posting assignments, sending messages, and creating and organizing Web sites. They facilitate assessment with a variety of online offerings, and they facilitate the integration of the World Wide Web into the curriculum. Educational portals are an important step in the movement toward online school communities.

Ex: America Online filters information from the Internet to eliminate material that is unsuitable for children.

Electronic Field Trips

Traditionally, field trips were planned group excursions to places of historic or cultural value, such as art museums, art galleries, and monuments. The purpose of these trips was to give students an opportunity for first-hand observation. Today, technology affords educators the opportunity to take students on electronic field trips, or virtual excursions. These "cyber-outings" are usually scheduled for a specified period of time, during which students can travel to various places around the world. There is an interactive exchange of information as students question experts and receive data for analysis.

Ex: MayaQuest '97—Students virtually accompanied the MayaQuest team of scientists as they took a bicycling expedition to research ancient Mayan civilization. The field trip was scheduled to last approximately one month. The team communicated with students from various countries around the globe as they toured various countries (Holzberg, 1996). Supplemental kits with video guides and student materials are available for purchase.

Experiential Learning

Experiential learning is knowledge gained through discovering new information and applying prior experiences or knowledge. Many educators view experiential learning as being more meaningful and significant because it usually involves practical applications that are closely associated with the real world (Rogers, 1969). Providing students with experiential or hands-on experience facilitates their connection between the real world and new information. Experiential learning dates back to John Dewey's work in 1938.

Ex: Computer simulations provide excellent opportunities for experiential learning.

Guided Imagery

Guided imagery is a technique for encouraging the body to relax and allowing the mind to be more receptive to information. The "altered" state that is achieved facilitates the processing of information that may often engage the senses. Although guided imagery is often used to release stress and facilitate healing, it can be a very effective medium for facilitating instruction through visualization.

Ex: A teacher could use guided imagery to take students on a visual-image trip into the past, helping them to envision a time and a place in history. She could, for example, encourage them to engage their senses of taste, touch, and hearing by suggesting that they taste the salty spray of the crashing, cold, ocean waters that have just washed over their sand-covered bodies as they lay on the hot, sandy beach of the new world.

Habit Formation

Habit formation is a response and an approach to moral or character education that involves helping children form behavioral habits that will create responsible model citizens. Habit formation is more effective if encouraged at an early age. It is an important component of contemporary character education programs. The difficulty of implementing habit formation lies in determining commonly agreed-upon behavior habits. On whose culture and whose values should these habits be based?

Ex: Teaching good habits is an important part of moral education in some elementary classrooms.

Homework Labs

Homework labs may be located in schools, libraries, churches, and almost any place that designates a meeting place for students to do homework or research projects. These labs may range from state-of-the-art computer centers to rooms with volunteers and minimal resources. Ideally, homework labs should be staffed with trained volunteers and provide computer equipment and print resources that will give students access to the most current, accurate information available. The staff should make maximum use of software programs to provide tutoring and assistance.

Ex: A library received a $6,000 homework center mini-grant to buy computers, books, and software. This equipment was used to teach children how to research homework projects. The library provided the trained volunteers.

Indirect Teaching

Indirect instruction, also called indirect teaching, is the transfer of knowledge by any means other than traditional direct instruction.

Ex: Indirect instruction may take any of the following forms: mentoring, tutoring, conducting workshops, training staff, making presentations, directing a thesis or dissertation, doing demonstrations, creating Web courses, and delivering public lectures.

Inquiry Learning

Inquiry learning is a problem-solving technique based on the scientific method. The first step is to define the problem. The teacher usually does this, but students also may pose the question. Proper structuring of questions is critical to inquiry learning. The problem can be open-ended (requiring creative, reflective answers using divergent thinking), closed (requiring definite answers using convergent thinking), active (requiring a search for the answer), or a combination of these problem types.

The second step involves gathering data and finding resources. The teacher functions as a facilitator, making sure that students have adequate resources to solve the problem. The third step includes developing a hypothesis, trying to determine causal relationships, and analyzing the data. The final step is to pause and reflect on the problem and engage in lively discussion. To solve the problem, students are encouraged to employ a variety of analytic strategies, such as classifying, categorizing, inferring, interpreting, and comparing (hydi Educational New Media Center, 1999). Students may use inductive or deductive inquiry. Inductive goes from specific information to a general rule, whereas deductive inquiry starts with a general rule and goes to specifics.

Ex: The class starts with the inquiry, "How can we simulate an erupting volcano using any of these food items and art materials?" The teacher gives students several foodstuffs that are safe to combine. They are free to construct any model of a volcano they want. The students may eventually discover that combining vinegar, baking powder, and soap creates a bubbling-over effect that could represent lava.

Interdisciplinary Unit

An interdisciplinary unit is an approach to teaching that involves combining several discrete academic disciplines such as science, social studies, art, math, and language into one instructional unit or section of a course. The unit usually focuses on a central theme that integrates all of the thematic contributions from various disciplines into a complete educational experience. Interdisciplinary units offer teachers great opportunities for collaboration, creativity, and using varied and innovative teaching strategies.

Ex: An interdisciplinary thematic unit on China might integrate math, art, language arts, social studies, and science. The teacher may introduce the abacus for the mathematics part of the unit. For the language arts strand, students might study the Chinese alphabet, write to Chinese pen pals, and use an electronic language translator to translate English words to Chinese, and vice versa. A trip to the Chinese Art section of the local museum, or a virtual visit to a famous museum on the Internet, or creating rice paper to make a Chinese watercolor would add an artistic activity to the unit. Students could study regional peoples, customs, and dialects for social studies. Examining the properties of different Chinese vegetables and cooking them would provide a scientific taste treat to complete the unit.

Learning Centers

Learning centers or interest centers are learning spaces that are devoted to planned activities, projects, and opportunities for self-instruction and practice. These centers are usually experiential, offering students "hands-on" experiences (Dewey, 1938). Discovery learning or inquiry learning centers are common contexts for learning centers. There are many benefits associated with learning centers. Students develop autonomy, self-direction, improved social interaction, and enhanced understanding of new and familiar topics. Centers offer a medium for limitless creativity and varied theme-based approaches to individualized instruction.

Ex: A learning assistance center for math may have calculators and a computer, which students can use to check their work and go online for tutorial sessions and assessment. Some programmed math instruction may be available online to help students pace their learning.

Lecture

Lecturing is the prototype or form of instruction that is most often associated with teaching. It usually involves organizing information on a particular topic to facilitate presentation by a teacher. It can be an effective technique for teaching large amounts of material or complex subjects in a short session. Prior to lectures, teachers gather relevant, essential information on a topic, arrange it in a logical sequence (such as objectives, content, and summary), and present it to a group. Lecturing can be boring and ineffective if the teacher talks for the entire session without using visual aids, media, or technology, or does not encourage student interaction.

Ex: Interactive lecturing is far more interesting and meaningful to students when they are allowed to interrupt a lecture and interject some of their ideas, criticisms, and arguments.

Literacy Skills

Literacy skills extend beyond knowing how to read and write in a language to being able to function in a literate environment and to take part in the social, economic, and political aspects of life. Effective literacy skills give people the resources to navigate a complex society to find employment, accumulate wealth, raise a family, secure an education, and make use of technology.

Ex: Literacy skills are critical for improving one's socioeconomic status. People must have the skills to apply for a position, negotiate salary, and understand job requirements. Once hired, they need literacy skills to determine the best strategies for accomplishing job tasks, to gauge and monitor progress and performance against performance of coworkers, to excel at their job, and to learn to negotiate raises and promotions. The needed skills clearly extend beyond reading and writing.

Literature Circles

Literature circles are small groups of students who meet regularly during class to discuss a book that they are reading. Each group has a different book. This group strategy uses a cooperative learning format, in which students rotate playing a different task role at different sessions. Role sheets can be effective for tracking roles, if their use is not overemphasized. Students are free to choose their reading materials and to develop topics for their discussions. Teachers function as facilitators, answering questions if necessary and encouraging students to have fun. Literature circles are an ongoing process. Once a group finishes discussing a book, students choose a new book and new groups are formed around the new books.

Ex: Martinez & Lopez (1999) conducted bilingual literature circles in their primary class. In this use of literacy circles, English- and Spanish-dominant students were placed in small groups to have a meaningful dialogue about books and critical societal issues that affect them. The purpose of the literature discussions was to challenge students' thinking and have them question their perceptions of reality.

Looping

Looping by any other name is merely the practice of keeping students and teachers together through two or more grade levels (Grant, 1996). It has been variously referred to as continuous learning, continuous progress, persisting groups, multiyear grouping, and teacher and student progression. The concept of looping made its debut in the early 1900s in a variety of forms. The unifying principle of these various forms was that long-term relationships between teachers and students were mutually beneficial. Looping has captured the interest of 21st-century educators, who embrace the logic and applaud the advantages of this practice. Looping gives teachers the advantage of knowing their students well, which helps them to better assess their students and devise ways to maximize student learning. With multiyear assignments, teachers can develop an instructional plan that capitalizes on knowledge gained from prior years. A major concern is that either a teacher or a student will be "stuck" in a bad situation for a longer time. To be effective, teachers who participate in looping should do so voluntarily and have a retreat clause that allows them to opt out of participating in future years. Students should be allowed to "retreat" and go to another class if it is not working for them.

Ex: My sixth-grade teacher kept our class until the eighth grade. He moved up a grade level as we moved up. We had the opportunity to explore some exciting science projects and activities over the years.

Mentoring

The mentoring process has evolved over the years to ease the transition of beginning teachers into the teaching profession. From day one of teaching, new teachers must assume the same duties and responsibilities as veteran teachers. The educational stakes are equally high for both new and experienced teachers. A mentor is usually a person with a degree of wisdom, experience, and knowledge to help the beginning teacher through difficult situations. Sweeny (1990) identified some of the forms that mentorship might assume:

- Orientation—helping the new teacher adjust to the new environment and job responsibilities
- Collaboration—working together to prepare for the beginning of school
- Sharing—exchanging ideas, methods, and techniques
- Jointly solving a problem—often relying on the mentor's expertise to find a solution
- Encouragement—building a strong professional and personal relationship to enhance the confidence of the novice teacher

The mentor relationship may be assigned or voluntary. Either way, personal compatibility and similar educational philosophies and beliefs will make the mentoring process more effective. The benefits of mentoring are many. For the student, mentoring minimizes the potentially negative effects of having an inexperienced teacher. For the novice teacher, mentoring enhances morale, eases transition, and accelerates acclimation to their new job. For mentoring to be effective, the relationship should be allowed to grow—or to dissolve, especially if it is not working for one or both of the parties involved.

Ex: In many school districts, a master teacher is assigned a novice teacher in an informal apprenticeship role. In some school districts, the mentor functions as an academic coach.

Mind Mapping

Mind mapping is a technique for graphically representing ideas and concepts that is based on association and emphasis, key elements involved in memorizing and retrieving information (Linguarama, 1999). The concept of mind mapping is a product of the research of Tony Buzan (1993), who is credited with the invention of mind mapping. In 1990 he registered the term, which is trademarked under the Buzan Organization. Haber's (1970) research on visual memory also contributed significantly to the development of mind mapping. Mind mapping is an effort to simulate a brain map or network of how information is processed. Like brain cells that branch out to form neural pathways and thereby form associations and links, the mind map starts with a subject and related ideas branch from it.

Presentations, informal talks, note taking, and lectures are some of the ways that mind mapping may be used. Actually, this technique is useful for anything requiring organization of thoughts. Mind mapping has superior advantage over other memory aids: It is brief and concise; it discourages reading in a presentation or talk; and it is flexible, making it easier to move among topics. Using this technique offers the presenter several advantages. Having to reduce ideas to one word facilitates not only the understanding of presentation material but also the memorization of key words necessary for information recall. Representing ideas graphically in a mind map makes them easier to remember because it is brief, organized, and stored in visual memory as a graphic. Our visual memory stores the information as a highly accurate representation of the original (photo-like), which facilitates recall (Linguarama, 1999).

Ex: Mind mapping can be computer-generated, taking advantage of various graphic effects such as highlights and animation, sound effects, and so on to enhance the mind map presentation.

Multisensory Instruction

Multisensory instruction is an approach that encourages the employment of all human senses to deliver instructional content to the brain. The five senses—auditory (hearing), visual (seeing), olfactory (smell), tactile (touch), and gustatory (taste)—each have a sensory modality or channel that receives, processes, stores, and retrieves the information when needed. The effectiveness of multisensory instruction is contingent upon engaging all the senses, or as many senses as possible, at the same time. Simultaneously engaging all senses maximizes the efficient processing, storing, and retrieval of information. Sensory engagement is essential for mastery learning.

Multisensory instruction is especially important for preschoolers. In Piaget's theory of cognitive development (1970), the first stage is the sensorimotor stage, when children rapidly learn about their environment through their senses. Children learn best when they can experience new things with all of their senses. Cooking affords a great opportunity to engage all of the senses, and young children love it.

Ex: Baking bread with young children is an easy way to engage most of the senses:

- Touch—kneading the bread dough, touching ingredients
- Sight—seeing the ingredients, watching the dough rise, watching it brown
- Smell—smelling the aroma of the baking bread
- Sound—hearing the mixing of the bread or the timer going off, signaling that the bread is ready
- Taste—enjoying the taste of fresh, warm bread with butter

Peer Mediation

Peer mediation is a conflict intervention strategy by which students mediate for their peers. This process involves helping students who are experiencing conflict to listen to each other's points of view. Typically, when these conflicts reach mediation, the people involved have resisted other attempts at resolving the conflict. Anyone can initiate a request for mediation—students, teachers, parents, and school personnel. In most cases, two or more student mediators under the supervision of a trained adult will work with each request for mediation. Mediation often provides a safe, supportive environment that is more conducive to honesty, responsibility, and reflection. Students work hard to reach a mutual agreement. If after a period of time it becomes apparent that the agreement is not working, adult intervention may be necessary.

Ex: In a schoolwide violence prevention program, a peer-mediation component significantly reduces incidences of violence by helping students resolve problems before they escalate to violence.

Phonics

Phonics is an approach to reading instruction that focuses on learning the names and sounds of the 26 letters of the alphabet, letter-sound relationships, combinations of sounds, and word sounds. There are two approaches to phonics instruction, implicit and explicit (Hiskes, 2000). Implicit phonics, most often taught in today's schools, stresses a whole-to-part approach in which the reader starts with the word and tries to guess it using configuration clues, context clues, beginning and ending letters, and so on. The explicit approach, which was used in teaching phonics years ago, involves moving from the smallest part to the whole. Students learn letters, then sounds, combinations, and words. Phonetic instruction may vary, but the following tasks are usually associated with explicit phonics (Hiskes, 2000):

a. Phonemic awareness, or the knowledge that each letter has its own speech sound
b. Knowledge of the interrelationships of letters and sounds; that there are approximately 44 sounds that can be combined in about 70 ways
c. Sounding out letters, blends, and words
d. Using configuration clues, tracing letters
e. Using decodable texts, or texts that reflect skills and knowledge previously taught, to reinforce skills and practice reading

Phonetic analysis was also important, whereby the child could break a word down to its smallest part and reconstruct it by knowing the speech sounds of consonants and vowels and how to blend the sounds back into words. Phonics is at the heart of the controversy commonly known as the reading wars, which pits the virtues of the phonetics instruction strategy against those of the whole-language approach.

Ex: "Hooked on Phonics" is a well-known commercial product designed to teach phonics at home. It features a set of audiotapes and instructions.

Portfolios

Portfolios are collections of representative samples of students' work, accomplishments, and performance. Portfolios are an alternate means of assessment that does not consume as much class time as traditional tests, but they do require considerable teacher effort. Portfolios give students an opportunity to participate in the assessment of their work, and to develop standards and criteria for evaluating the quality of work. The portfolio may contain writing samples, drawings, tape recordings of oral reading, peer-review materials, science experiments, videos of performances, and photos of projects or exhibits. Ideally, portfolios should include some form of recorded, systematic observation. Grace (1992) suggests the following forms of observation: (a) anecdotal records or nonjudgmental notes of children's activities, (b) a checklist or inventory based on instructional objectives, (c) rating scales, (d) open-ended questions and requests for information, and (e) screening tests or ascertainments of prior learning, skills, and strengths. One drawback of portfolios is that parents may be wary of them if they are used in lieu of traditional tests.

Ex: A science portfolio might contain a photograph of a science fair exhibit, written reports of experiments, a video of the student performing an experiment, data logs, an award for a science project, a teacher's anecdotal records of observations of student inquiry behaviors, and a student's evaluation of some work samples.

Premack Principle

The Premack principle, named for David Premack (1965), is a behavioristic method for establishing effective reinforcement and controlling behavior. The premise is to make participation in a preferred, desirable behavior contingent on the completion of a less desirable behavior. A teacher is using the Premack principle if she tells students that they cannot go out for recess until they finish cleaning out their desks. The assumption is that recess is desirable and cleaning desks is less desirable.

Ex: Ranked reinforcement—Teachers can rank student activities in an order that students would perceive as ranging from very desirable to undesirable. Teachers can make participation in the desirable activities contingent on the completion of less desirable activities.

Rehearsal

Rehearsal is an educational practice that dates back to late 19th-century teaching. It is synonymous with "learning by heart" or rote memorization. It is an exercise of memory with a goal of total recall of the memorized subject matter. This practice is still used today; it is now referred to as maintenance rehearsal, which is simply repeating information repeatedly to create a durable memory that can be recalled. Craik and Lockhart (1972) proposed an additional type of rehearsal (elaborative rehearsal) in their theory of levels of processing in memory. Elaborative rehearsal is the act of associating the subject matter with something meaningful. These authors proposed that elaborative rehearsal invokes a deeper level of semantic processing, which could result in durable memories that may facilitate the ease of recall.

Ex: Elaborative rehearsal seeks to add meaning to items to be remembered, to make them easier to recall. When I wanted to remember a numeric code for the copier, the numbers I chose were the date of my birthday along with the number of children I had. This association attached meaning to a seemingly meaningless set of numbers. I always remembered the copy code after this elaborative form of rehearsal.

Role-Play

Role-play is usually a simulation of some real-world activity or situation. It allows participants to temporarily assume roles in a mini-drama format to practice interpersonal skills, interviewing skills, advising or counseling skills, or other similar skills in a relatively safe setting. A drawback that can undermine the effectiveness of this technique is participant reluctance. Participants may be uncomfortable revealing their thoughts and actions for public scrutiny and evaluation. Being clear about the use of role-play and offering a tactful way for those who dislike the activity to opt out of it will minimize the effects of reluctant participants.

Ex: To practice their counseling skills, participants assume the roles of client or therapist. The role-play may be videotaped for debriefing and discussion.

Rote Memorization

Learning by rote is a memorization process through which the student "learns" or remembers information by repeating it many times, without necessarily understanding or comprehending its meaning. In the past, teachers believed that if students could regurgitate the information correctly, they had learned the material. This passive teaching practice is a legacy of the Early National period of American education (circa 1776–1840) when mental discipline theory, which stressed using "the mind as a mental muscle," was popular. During that time, students were required to memorize and recite.

Although more contemporary theories and practices have demonstrated the value of learning that is grounded in meaningful contexts, schools still rely on rote memorization of certain facts and principles without connecting that information to its use in a real-world context. Consequently, rote memorization is less likely to promote information transfer (Institute for Learning Sciences, 1994).

Ex: I observed preschoolers repeatedly reciting the names of geometric figures. The teacher held up the picture, and the group said the names together. These geometric figures were not limited to the square, triangle, circle, and rectangle; also included were the rhombus, trapezoid, parallelogram, and other advanced figures. It was impressive to see the children identify all of the figures, but they did not understand what the figures meant or how they were used in the real world.

Rubrics

A rubric is an assessment tool that lists performance standards and expectations for students. It is a scoring guide that features qualitative or quantitative scores, and in some cases both. Definitions of rubrics vary. Basically, they are guidelines for assessment, stating what is being assessed and what criteria will be used to make the assessment. Rubrics are reminiscent of instructional objectives. Objectives are statements of expected outcomes, and rubrics are assessments of actual educational outcomes. Rubrics give students a clear understanding of what is expected of them.

Ex: Table 1.2 is a rubric detailing course requirements and grading.

Scaffolding

Conceptually, scaffolding is a technique of giving students support that can be likened to the metal scaffolds used for support on construction sites. With scaffolding, adults provide just the right amount of support at just the right time (Wood, Bruner, & Ross, 1976). Support may be in the form of explanations, hints, reminders, details, demonstrations, visual and verbal cues, prompts, and so on. The goal is to help students become independent learners by providing needed support while the child is in a zone of proximal development (ZPD), a place where they cannot solve a problem without adult assistance or help from a knowledgeable peer (Wertsch, 1991). Scaffolding is most effective if it is gradually withdrawn as the child masters the problem, or increased if the student appears to have difficulty.

Table 1.2 A Modified Rubric for Course Requirements and Points

Assignment	Expected Activities	Possible Points	Your Actual Points
Test #1	Review chps. 1–4; class notes & discussions; handouts; Essays from supplemental text	60 points	
Midterm (Test #2)	Chapters 1–6 Essays from supplemental text	60 points	
Test #3	Chapter 8–9 Essays from supplemental text	60 points	
Final	Review chps. 9–15; study guide; review sheet; class notes Essays from supple-mental text	100 points	
Study Guide	Complete the study guide	10 points	
Internet computer assignment	Research assigned educa-tional topic	10 points	
Total		300 points	
Grade		300–268 = A 267–239 = B 238–200 = C 199–169 = D 168–0 = F	Your Grade =

Ex: A student is attempting a task and is experiencing difficulty. The teacher offers some verbal clues or hints. The student moves closer to mastery. The student uses private speech or self-talk to give herself clues, thereby reducing the need for adult assistance. At that point, the teacher should continue to monitor the situation but refrain from offering hints, thereby effectively reducing the scaffolding.

Simulation

Simulation is an experiential problem solution process that gives learners an opportunity to solve problems in a simulated or representative real-life context. Simulations can mirror almost any real-life situation using an appropriate model. Space expeditions, job shadowing, fighting an epidemic, or building a city are examples of some life situations modeled by simulations. Such simulations can be very useful if the real-world setting is too dangerous, too costly, or too remote to allow for firsthand experience. Many simulations encourage development of critical thinking, problem-solving skills, and analytical thinking skills. They can be individualized to meet students' needs. They offer immediate feedback and follow-up as they involve students in active, participatory learning.

Ex: Computer simulations on CD-ROM are very popular formats. SetQuest Interactive is a computer simulation that lets students participate in a career simulation in the classroom (Dillon, 1998). It simulates several science, engineering, and technology careers.

Socratic Method

Socratic pedagogy is a method of teaching that uses dialogue and questions to lead a learner to appropriate answers for a particular problem. This technique dates back to Socrates, who reportedly taught his students by questions only, which is the Socratic method in its purest form. Today, about two thousand years later, the Socratic method is less pure, allowing more dialogue and fewer questions. For Socratic dialogue to occur, questions should be open-ended rather than requiring an answer of yes or no.

The Socratic method is preferable to lecture because it engages students' minds and facilitates understanding. The teacher acts as a facilitator to help students use their intellectual abilities to construct meaning, dissect and reconstruct ideas, and to create new ideas. Neumayr (2000) contends that the Socratic method is preferable to lecture because dialogue engages the mind in ways that lecture never could. He believes that the Socratic method results in better retention because ideas that students work out for themselves are more likely to be retained. One drawback of this method is that students may get stuck and be unable to figure out an appropriate response to a question. If that happens, an explanation or some prompting may be necessary. Another limitation is the time involved beforehand in designing a sequence of questions that will lead to a correct response.

Ex: Rick Garlikov (1999) used the Socratic method to teach binary arithmetic (a base-two system of arithmetic that uses 1 and 0) to a third-grade class. Garlikov concluded that his method was effective because 19 of 22 students were very involved and appeared to have absorbed all of the material. The classroom teacher concurred with his results.

SQ4R

SQ4R is an acronym for a study strategy designed to help students make more effective and productive use of their textbooks. It means S (survey) and Q (question), 4R's (read, recite, reflect or record, review). To survey is to preview the book or examine all parts of it—the table of contents, objectives, outlines, summaries, and so on. Students are encouraged to formulate questions for self-instruction and to facilitate interactive reading. They can look for the answers to their formulated questions to make the reading interactive and more meaningful. Reflecting or thinking about the material can also make the reading more meaningful. Reciting, self-testing, or explaining to others helps to organize information. Review is essential for meaningful rehearsal and retention.

Ex: SQ4R or one of its derivatives (SQ3R or PQ4R) can be found in most textbooks on study skills.

Team Teaching

Team teaching is a useful deviation from the traditional one-teacher classroom. This approach to teaching coordinates teacher ideas, activities, and interests to meet the diverse needs of students and enrich their learning experiences. Team teaching is positive in that it exposes students to different perspectives, teaching styles, and teaching approaches. The more diversity among teachers, the richer the offering. Teachers' roles on the team vary as determined by their level of expertise, training, and experience (Gable & Manning, 1999).

The negatives of team teaching, inherent in that diversity, invite conflict. Schamber (1999) offers a number of admonitions that if adhered to may increase the effectiveness of teaming. She emphasizes the importance of avoiding practices that erode the level of group trust, such as situations in which only a few team members participate in discussions and make decisions. For teaming to be effective and successful, schools must give teachers time to work together to plan for the needs of students. Students and teachers will reap the benefits of this administrative support in the form of better teaching and learning.

Ex: One variation of team teaching is teacher collaboration, in which two or three teachers designate an allotted amount of time for teaming. They divide their classes and teach various subjects (Horowitz, 1997). Another variation is interdisciplinary teaming, which is comprised of three to five teachers with diverse interests and expertise.

Time Capsule

The time capsule is a hands-on instructional technique or device for recording historical events. It gives students an opportunity to actively participate in making history by capturing a moment in time. Students may use plastic soda bottles or more elaborate containers as long as they are waterproof, durable, and protect the contents. Time capsules are usually a collection of artifacts and memorabilia that reflect a certain time period. This collection should include only high-quality items that can withstand the conditions they are likely to be subjected to in a capsule. The time capsule technique is useful for teaching the concept of historical change, for comparing and contrasting historical periods, and for testing hypotheses and predictions of historical outcomes.

Ex: A class created a video time capsule of their experiences and interests by using scripted video segments of their sports activities, pep rallies, concerts, assemblies, and so on. The instructional purpose was to use time capsules to enhance literacy skills (Lonberger & Lonberger, 1995).

TouchMath

TouchMath is a multisensory approach to teaching basic numerical recognition and math computation skills. Janet Bullock (Innovative Learning Concepts, 1999) developed this system in 1976 while attempting to offer math remediation to some of her sixth-grade students. TouchMath is multisensory in that it uses a sensory rehearsal strategy that combines visual, vocal, auditory, and tactile cues to facilitate the acquisition and retention of numbers. Students look at the number and say the number as they touch it and trace it.

The TouchMath system uses a specified number of Touchpoints that corresponds to the value of that number. Touchpoints may be single or double. A single Touchpoint or dot is counted once. A double Touchpoint is a dot with a ring around it, and it is counted twice. A combination of single and double Touchpoints is used to represent the value of each number. Digits 1–5 use a single Touchpoint, and digits 6–9 use double points or a combination of single and double points.

The TouchMath approach is used extensively in special education for students who are below grade level, and for math remediation. Although it is an ingeniously simplistic method, it is highly effective. Most students learn the numbers in 1 week, or in some cases 1 day. Many students have mastered basic computation skills in about 4 months with about 97 percent accuracy (Innovative Learning Concepts, 1999). The TouchMath system is available in a kit of blackline reproducible masters. Teachers are free to reuse these masters as often as they like. Puzzles, posters, and various other teaching aids are available in the kit. Training in the use of the TouchMath approach is available as a videotape seminar.

Ex: Figure 1.2 illustrates TouchMath Touchpoints.

Figure 1.2   Single and Double Touchpoints for Numbers 1–9

Vertical Teams

Vertical teams are planning teams comprised of teachers, administrators, counselors, and other school personnel who work together to improve student achievement. The concept is vertical in that schools are linked from elementary school to college, forming a vertical structure of lower to higher schools. A basic goal of vertical teaming is to facilitate the smooth transition of students through the system. The teams work together to align objectives, standards, curriculum assessments, and whatever else is needed at each level, from pre-K through college. Student progress is measured by benchmarks agreed upon by the vertical team. If a student has missed important benchmarks, the vertical team is committed to mobilizing the entire community to provide the necessary resources and assistance to improve student achievement.

Ex: Faculty from the University of California, Santa Cruz work in a Partnership Schools Program with administrators, teachers, and staff from feeder schools to facilitate student progress toward the completion of benchmarks.

Virtual Reality

Virtual reality is an interactive computer-generated environment that uses technology to create an illusion of reality. The participant wears a helmet-shaped apparatus that uses small computer screens juxtaposed before the participant's eyes to simulate stereoscopic vision. Sensors that transmit information on body movement give an interactive effect. Sometimes audio, video, 3-D graphics, or scent may be used to enhance the realism of the experience. Virtual reality is new to education, but efforts are under way to develop new instructional uses for it. It should be very useful for virtual education or virtual classrooms used in online education systems.

Ex: The Center for Human Simulation provides surgical training using anatomical images and virtual reality simulators in a medical education program. Such a system allows for better visualization of surgical procedures and offers a preview of consequences of decisions.

Zone of Proximal Development

A basic tenet of Vygotsky's (1987) sociocultural learning theory is that we generate knowledge in a social context, through interaction with others. The zone of proximal development (ZPD) is merely the gap between what a child can do alone and what a child can do with the support of clues, reminders, encouragement, and other forms of assistance from an adult or knowledgeable peer. Some problems may be very challenging and just above the child's level of development. An adult can help the child solve the problem through prompts and then back off when the child seems to be at a point where she can solve the problem alone. Teachers can offer demonstrations or further explanations to facilitate the problem-solving process. This type of assistance is referred to as scaffolding.

Ex: A child in a math challenge program is learning basic algebra. She is having difficulty understanding that the operations change when moved to the opposite side of the equation. The teacher offers some assistance. "Let's think of the equal sign (=) as a little bridge. When a number crosses the bridge, its sign is automatically changed to the opposite sign. For example, $3x + 2 = 8$. The 2 travels across the bridge and becomes -2. So, $3x = 8 - 2$, and now $3x = 6$."

"I see it." the child responds. "Next I will have to take the 3 across the bridge, and it will have a division sign, and . . . I think I can finish the problem."

"Great!"

2

Programs

Educational programs are a system of services or projects, usually designed to meet an academic need.

"I can suck pudding up my nose and blow it out the corner of my eye, but they still won't put me in the gifted program at school!"

Accelerated Reader

The Accelerated Reader program began as a response to the need for an educational initiative. Chevron's president was dismayed at the shortfall of qualified workers. Sixty percent of new applicants lacked basic reading and math skills. Current research indicates that 40–60 million adults are reading at the lowest levels of literacy (Kozol, 1985; Tozer, 1998).

The president of Chevron wanted to address the problem on a broader, systemic basis. In 1988, he challenged his company to come up with a plan for providing meaningful, effective assistance to the apparently unsuccessful K–12 educational system in the United States. He gave the team three objectives:

- Identify key educational problems facing the U.S. system.
- Examine how other companies, including Chevron, are addressing them.
- Find a suitable program.

The president sought to fund a program that could help to move more at-risk students into the educational mainstream by accelerating their achievement at the middle school level.

The Chevron team delineated the following criteria for program success and subsequent funding:

- Offer true innovative change or reform rather than a simple modification of an existing system.
- Address a widely recognized, critical problem that has resisted solution.
- Have specific, measurable, and attainable objectives and goals.
- Effectively use both human and financial capital.
- Strategically employ early intervention, teacher training, and parental involvement as major considerations in the project. (Levin, 1991)

Henry Levin's Accelerated Schools program was chosen to serve as Chevron's educational initiative. It met all the criteria for success. The program was broadly based on three schoolwide principles (Levin, 1991): (a) having a cohesive, unified effort of family, school, and community working toward improving the academic ability of at-risk students and bringing them into the educational mainstream, (b) sharing responsibility and accountability among designated staff, students, and parents, (c) acknowledging and building on the strengths of at-risk students and their cultures.

The Accelerated Reader is a reading management program used in the Accelerated Schools program. It is a computer-based tool that provides for self-paced, individualized instruction and student choice. It features software that gives educators an authentic, timely snapshot of accurate, student-specific performance information. The program claims to be as easy as ABC, because it's based on three simple steps. Step one: Each student chooses a book from a specified selection of books. According to the current catalog, approximately 27,000 titles are available, ranging from first to twelfth grade. The level of difficulty also varies within grade level. Step two: Students read the book and take a literacy test that is available online, to assess their knowledge of the book content. The computer scores the test and immediately responds with feedback and incentive points that are based on the length and level of difficulty of the book. Step three: The teacher receives quick, accurate assessment information for each student. Student progress may be displayed in chart, graph, or report form.

The program uses award points to increase the likelihood that students will read more books and increase the level of difficulty of those books. A Texas teacher says students redeem their points for merchandise such as pens, posters, and toys on Accelerated Reader (AR) shopping days. Local merchants usually donate the prizes. The controversy over the effects of intrinsic versus extrinsic rewards is evident in the Accelerated Reader program. The source of controversy is awarding points for reading books. Giving rewards fosters extrinsic motivation, which is less desirable than the intrinsic motivation fostered by encouraging students to read for the sheer joy of reading itself.

Kohn (1993) opposes extrinsic motivators, saying they dehumanize students. Oldfather and Dahl (1995) contend that it may be difficult to separate intrinsic and extrinsic motivators because one often acts as a means to the other's end. Proponents such as Cameron and Pierce (1994) conducted a meta-analytic study of 96 studies of motivation and found convincing evidence that extrinsic motivators may enhance rather than extinguish intrinsic motivation. Previous studies have proposed that extrinsic motivators diminish intrinsic motivation.

The goals of the Accelerated Reader program are to help students to read not only more books, but more challenging books. An affective goal of the program is to encourage a love of reading and lifelong learning.

Grade Levels   The Accelerated Reader program can be implemented on a classwide, schoolwide, or districtwide basis for grades pre-K through 12. Schools select an appropriate kit as determined by their resources, goals, and interests.

Materials   Three kits are available:

- The Starter, with 4 titles per disk (up to 200 quizzes)
- The Economy, with 20 titles per disk (up to 1000 quizzes)
- The Super Kit, with 20 titles per disk (up to 1000 quizzes) plus bonus items

All kits include the following materials:

- Accelerated Reader Software (online practice quizzes)
- Network-wide school site license

- Software manual
- A 12-month expert support plan
- "Getting started" booklet

Teachers can expand kits by ordering more quizzes and more student capacity. More than 27,000 titles are available. Books are usually kept in media centers and are distinguished from other books by a logo sticker. The company offers training for teachers.

Program Effectiveness There is overwhelming evidence that the Accelerated Reader program is effective. It is being used in over 50,000 schools in the United States. Studies indicate that students participating in the Accelerated Reader program had improved reading comprehension and attitudes about reading (Scott, 1999; Vollands, Topping, & Evans, 1996). Various independent research reports supplied by the company show that Accelerated Reader does improve test scores. The program appears to meet its goals and objectives of encouraging learners to read more and better books.

Benefits Reports indicate that the students are excited and motivated by the program.

This definitely encourages reading! Children are self-motivated to do their best and seek out additional reading materials. (Teacher of the Year, Missouri)

Concerns

Causes many students not to read books that are not on the list. (Teacher of the Year, Iowa)

Barriers to Implementation To implement the program, a considerable investment in software and books is needed. The kits cost several thousand dollars. Affluent schools with a large budget can afford a larger selection of titles than can less-affluent schools. Consequently, schools with limited resources may not see the same benefits or dramatic gains that may be apparent in affluent schools.

Reflections The Accelerated Reader program is influenced by several learning theories. It is cognitive in its focus on comprehension and recall. The rewarding of reading points is primarily behaviorist, reflecting Skinnerian operant conditioning through positive reinforcement (Skinner, 1953). Social learning is evidenced in teachers and students modeling reading behavior and encouraging imitation by sharing stories (Bandura, 1986). Vygotsky's (1987) notion of a zone of proximal development (ZPD) is apparent in the program goals of helping students read more and better books. Students also are encouraged to read more difficult books. Teachers use diagnostic feedback from the quizzes to facilitate student learning. They work with students within their ZPD to help them manage difficult reading assignments.

Alternative Education

Alternative education, or alternative schooling, began as the "free schools" movement of the 1960s. Initially, alternative schools were found primarily in private settings. The concept is now embraced by the public sector. Alternative education programs can best be defined in obscure terms of separateness, learning environment, and variation. The one constant in their definition is that they vary in purpose and objectives.

Alternative schooling originated as an educative counter to the precipitously high incidence of students who are not enrolled in school and have not graduated. According to the National Center for Educational Statistics (in De La Rosa, 1998, p. 268), 3.9 million 16- to 24-year-olds are not enrolled and have not graduated from high school. One goal of alternative schooling is to change the student—and keep the student in school—by changing the educational setting. A second goal is to empower students who are poor, at risk of dropping out, or otherwise disenfranchised.

An argument against alternative schools is that they usually cost more per pupil than traditional schools, which probably diverts resources from other schools (Soliel, 1999). Another argument is that alternative schools do not have a clear focus or a clearly delineated purpose. The purpose of a school could be to educate, enrich, accelerate, reform, rehabilitate, discipline, empower, or restore. The school format also varies. They may be magnet schools, afterschool programs, charter schools, career-oriented, dropout prevention, or detention centers (Soliel, 1999). Alternative schools with a punitive, disciplinary focus are viewed least favorably. Critics are concerned that this type of schooling reaps few positive long-term gains or outcomes (Raywid, 1994).

Raywid (1990, 1994) has identified three types of schools based on their characteristics. Type I schools have an educative focus and offer innovative curriculums and a variety of instructional options. Type II schools are reform oriented with an intent to isolate or reform disruptive or truant students. Type III schools have a therapeutic focus, with an intent to restore or rehabilitate students. This type of school serves as a refuge for students with behavioral, social, or emotional problems

Grade Levels   Alternative schools are typically secondary.

Barriers to Implementation   A lack of clarity of purpose can confuse implementation. A lack of funding may force organizations to reallocate monies targeted for other programs. Difficulty determining an appropriate organizational format and purpose may make it difficult to match student problems with the appropriate setting. A committed, qualified staff is critical to program success. A lack of space could be a problem because most alternative schools are off campus or in separate, smaller buildings. Parents must buy into the need for alternative schooling for their children.

Program Effectiveness The overall impression of alternative schools is divided. Educators believe that schools with a positive focus are more effective, and that schools with a punitive focus are less effective. They believe that test scores improve for students in Type I schools, but not for students in the Type II or III school. But educators also believe that Type II and III schools show some success in GED competition, remediation, and personal development.

Alternative schools are now a worldwide movement (Raywid, 1998). Overall, they seem to have a positive effect on students. Some educators believe alternative schooling enhances student self-esteem and motivation. The program appears to meet its objectives—students show signs of change and believe they can return to school in the traditional setting. Some believe that these programs help students learn their capacity.

Benefits In alternative schools, students with emotional problems get a psychological time-out that includes help from outside sources. For some students, nontraditional schools are their last chance to pursue an education. Schools with interesting, challenging curriculum are great motivators. These curricula are more personalized and individualized, and in some cases offer tailored remediation. Alternative schools are smaller and offer the student more one-on-one opportunities and improved parent-teacher communication.

Alternative schooling does remove potential trouble and allow for more individual instruction. (Teacher of the Year, New Jersey)

Helps students [who are] unable to function in traditional school setting or have special needs. (Teacher of the Year, Hawaii)

Concerns Some educators and students perceive the work in the punitive alternative schools as less challenging or too easy (Kallio & Sanders, 1999). Others worry that the students are isolated or segregated.

Can cause isolation. (Teacher of the Year, New Jersey)

Must have as its prime objective to return the student to the mainstream. There is only one world to live in. Don't allow the alternative to present an alternative to normal society. (Teacher of the Year, Montana)

Reflections DeCharms's (1976) origin vs. pawn theory may explain some of the variance in the success rate of different types of alternative schools. In the Type I school students function as origins, acting as if control of their behavior originates from within them. Rotter (1966) would call this an internal locus of control, which is good and empowering for students. They are successful because they attend these schools by choice, and they believe that they can achieve. These students appropriately attribute their failures and success to their efforts and abilities.

On the other hand, students in the Type II schools function more like pawns who believe they are controlled by external sources, creating in them an external locus of control (Rotter, 1966). These students are forced to attend school, and behavior modification strategies are imposed on them for what are often temporary or fleeting results. Unfortunately, this disempowerment is manifested in lowered achievement scores; increased absenteeism; and no reduction in suspension, expulsion, or dropout rates in this student population (Soliel, 1999).

Balanced Literacy

The sensational exposé on widespread illiteracy that was rampant early in the 20th century marked the onset of the famed "reading wars" that would rage on for decades. The public outcry was that schools were not teaching children how to read—who or what was to blame? Over the years, the gradual emergence of reading techniques based on various philosophies sparked the controversy known as the reading wars. At the center of the reading wars debate was the issue of which reading technique was effective and which was ineffective—which was to blame for America's high rate of illiteracy? The "look-say," or "sight-word," method of reading instruction was popular from about 1940 to 1970. This method of instruction involved teaching frequently used words, and teaching children to memorize them and recognize them on sight. In some cases, students guessed words from a picture or context.

From the 1970s until about 1990, phonics was king. Phonics teaches blending the phonetic sounds and syllables of the English language together into words. Phonics was the predecessor, and a respected method of teaching reading, but was not without its critics. During the 1990s, "whole language" enjoyed popularity. After a few years, it was attacked and criticized to a battle cry of "back to basics." Amidst the finger pointing of proponents and opponents of both whole language and phonics, the question loomed, which was better? Phonics? Whole language? Around the late 1990s, educators started entertaining the possibility that it could be both. Ausselin (1999) proposed combining whole language and phonics into a balanced reading program, referred to as balanced literacy. Balanced literacy is a recognition that the two approaches to reading are different, yet complementary, and when used appropriately can yield very effective results. Balanced literacy involves the integration of listening and speaking within an independent or group reading and writing format.

Benefits

Students are provided multiple paths to learning. (Teacher of the Year, Iowa)

Our language arts program in Virginia Beach is based on the belief that any literacy must be a balanced one: shared reading and writing with much modeling by the teacher, guided reading in small groups using leveled texts, independent reading. I have surveyed most mid-sized to large school systems in Virginia within the past month and almost everyone has moved to a balanced literacy approach. The key is teacher modeling and finding the instructional and independent reading level of the student. We have mandated that all teachers in our elementary schools be trained in balanced literacy and guided reading instruction. (Teacher of the Year, Virginia)

Character Education

Thomas Lickona (2000), director of the Center of the 4th and 5th R's, defines character education as a purposeful intent to help people understand and respect core ethical values. The question is, what are the core ethical values? Of course, the answer to that question is relative. A variety of definitions seem to center around an ill-defined core of ethical principles. However, the Character Education Partnership (2000) has identified values such as respect, responsibility, honesty, fairness, and caring as core ethical values.

Character Education is thought to date back to Socrates, when educational goals were to produce students who were "good and smart." Attempts to produce students who were both good and smart are evidenced in the curriculum of old, which featured courses in civics and gave grades in citizenship. A split in the focus on creating students who were both good and smart manifested during the late 1800s and carried over into the 1900s.

During the 1920s and 1930s, John Dewey was given credit for the Character Education movement. He wrote extensively on character education, advocating strong moral character. Other educators wanted more focus on academics. The latter faction received needed support for their cause when Edward Thorndike directed a study indicating that character education had limited effects on children's behavior (Cunningham, 1997).

Consequently, character education lost its luster and was forced into hibernation for several years. Escalating school violence, and antisocial behaviors and attitudes of young people, suggest the presence of a deep moral decay in our society and have kindled renewed interest in character education.

Grade Levels   Pre-K through 12

Materials and Procedures   Character education is free, or there may be a nominal charge. In some cases, materials for starting a character education program are available for about $35. The price varies as more components are added.

Barriers to Implementation   A major obstacle to establishing a character education program is determining what character education looks like.

Many educators lack a clear sense of what should be done in a character education program. Religious beliefs, cultural mores, and societal conventions are complex variables that contribute to the multidimensionality of character education. Another problem lies in finding strong leadership. DeRoche (2000) believes that a character education program will fade away without a strong leader. It is all but impossible to have value-free education. Teachers may inadvertently impose their views, values, and beliefs on lesson content and classroom interactions. The big question in character education is at what level should the program try to reach consensus on core values? Should it be at the community level, district level, state level, or school level?

Concerns   Parents are concerned that their children may be indoctrinated with doctrine and principles that do not reflect the family's values and beliefs.

This should be taught at home. (Teacher of the Year, New Jersey)

Some parents perceive this as teaching morals and do not support it. (Teacher of the Year, Mississippi)

Benefits   The Association for Supervision and Curriculum Development advocates that character education helps to reunite the timeless goals of Socrates in helping students to become both good and smart.

Teaches responsibility for one's actions. Teaches respect for others. (Teacher of the Year, Mississippi)

Provides a common language, modeling, and opportunities for participation. (Teacher of the Year, Iowa)

Helps students learn appropriate behaviors. (Teacher of the Year, Guam)

Classroom teachers have always taught character education ("be nice to your neighbor," "take turns," punctuality, citizenship, honesty, etc.). Good principals have always taught character education, too. It really is nothing new. (Teacher of the Year, Oregon)

Reflections   I am dismayed at the moral and spiritual decay that is so apparent in many of our children. It seems that arguments over what spiritual and moral food should be fed to our young people have created an impasse that has resulted in the spiritual and moral starvation of youth. I agree with the Character Education Partnership that it is imperative for educators to find common ground, in terms of the core ethical principles that should be taught, and do something. Haynes (2000) is confident that this can be done, but cautions that the common core of values should be both rooted in constitutional principles and free from religious indoctrinations.

Charter Schools

The concept of charter schools is something of an oxymoron, because they are private schools that are publicly supported (Wronkovich, 2000). The state of Minnesota was the first to enact a charter school law that allowed teachers and parents to "charter" their vision of a school that would be unencumbered by state rules and regulations. Charter school law would enable them to create schools that would more effectively serve the needs of the immediate population and subsequently improve education. The charter schools are a movement toward school reform that focuses on promoting more parent and teacher influence, using innovation to improve education, improving accountability, and encouraging student autonomy and choice (Rose, 1999).

The increasing popularity of charter schools has fostered their growth at all grade levels and in varying formats. A charter school may be a separate school with separate funding, or it can be a school within a school. Proponents of charter schools envision an economic model of supply and demand to drive the quality of the academic program. The quality is measured by test scores. If the quality is good, the schools enjoy success. If it is not good, they'll fail and lose their funding—this is a powerful incentive to offer a high-quality program. This model of supply and demand also provides a measure of accountability. Charter schools are usually formed by a group of teachers, parents, and/or community leaders motivated by a desire to make substantive contributions to educational reform.

Anyone can write a charter, but they must secure the signatures of 50 percent of teachers at a school or a minimum of 10 percent of the teachers in the school district that will receive the charter submission. The timeline for approval of a charter is from 30 to 60 days. Charter schools are usually nonprofit ventures; they must be nondenominational, they cannot discriminate, and they cannot charge tuition. Students cannot be mandated to attend these schools.

Barriers to Implementation   Many charter schools will attract less experienced teachers because they usually pay less than their host school district. Educators complain that most company sponsors have their own vision of what it takes to run a good charter school. The company's ideas and motives frequently conflict and violate the initiatives of promoting parental influence and participation that underlie the charter school concept.

Concerns   As with most new ventures, concerns abound. Low teacher salaries foster concerns about being able to attract experienced, capable teachers. Per-pupil expenditure is lower than in traditional nonprofit schools, which is an important concern. According to Rose (1999), charter schools cut per-pupil costs by spending less on students and cutting faculty salaries to half of what their counterparts in traditional schools earn. Charter schools must have high scores as evidence of their success or risk losing their funding. An unpleasant rumor and cause for concern is that some charter schools may be discouraging or counseling our non-English-speaking, minority, or special needs children to avoid the risk of lowered test scores. Rose (1999) contends that charter schools must have strong, effective academic programs in light of the movement to end social promotion; their students must also show evidence of competence and mastery of basic skills to graduate. The fact that anyone can start a charter school raises concerns about that person's qualifications and effectiveness. Current checks and balances in the start-up process may minimize those concerns.

Despite the concerns surrounding charter schools, many educators believe that these schools have potential. Long waiting lists at some schools may attest to the effectiveness and desirability of charter schools (Rose, 1999). Farius and Tatum (2001) see many benefits of charter schools. They believe these schools open the doors of opportunity for all families, not just affluent ones, and that they attract funding and interest that ultimately benefit public schools. Charter schools have been accused of taking the focus off public schools and of skimming the "cream" of public school-children.

> As long as money to charter schools does not strip money from generic schools, I support the idea. If all students are given the opportunity to select, I support the idea. There need to be alternatives that speak to each learner. (Teacher of the Year, Oregon)

Reflections   When schools change their focus to making a profit, their missions and agendas are inextricably altered. As in corporations, the pursuit of profit by schools limits the reception to human error and individual needs. To make a profit, the primary focus must be on the organization's needs. A bottom-line, profit-oriented environment is less conducive to the humanistic, constructivist approaches to education that are so needed today. Recent changes in academic policy advocate an end to social promotion and increased demands for students to demonstrate competence and mastery in academic skills. Those changes suggest an end to frenzied over-reliance on test scores and demand experienced teachers, a well-articulated instructional program, and engaging pedagogy. Inadequate resources, inexperienced teachers, inaccurate educational visions, and ineffective models of educational programs may be fodder for failure. Hopefully, the promise of success for charter schools outweighs the risks of failure. The children of this new venture may not bear the burden of failure well in our test-score-driven environment.

Chicago Math

Chicago Math, or the Everyday Mathematics Program, is a product of the University of Chicago's effort to provide a new reform-oriented K–12 curriculum. Historically, the initiative was inspired and directed by research from the 1980s, which suggested that all 5- to 9-year-olds, regardless of economic status, had untapped capabilities that could benefit from reform. Some guiding principles of this project are that teacher collaboration is essential for success, and that a math curriculum should proceed from the bottom up from one year to the next, to create a smooth transition based on the child's successful experiences in the previous year.

For some educators, this bridging of early experiences and ideas to more mature ideas is reminiscent of the "spiral curriculum." The originators prefer to think of their approach as consistent follow-up, and a variety of experiences are based on a "two-year rule," which suggests that a concept be introduced informally for two years before it is actually studied. They also embrace "the five-exposure rule," which dictates that a concept be practiced in five or more settings to facilitate learning. The curriculum encourages a hands-on approach (Bell, 1995). This program is highly controversial. It is based on the whole math concept that is rooted in the "new-new math" movement of the 1980s. Whole math is also referred to as connected math, or fuzzy math. The math reform effort began in 1989, initiated by a recommendation from the National Council of Teachers of Mathematics to overhaul the current approach to teaching mathematics in order to curb falling test scores and students' poor performance in math. This new-new math would go beyond the new math goals of shifting from rote memorization. It would include making math more meaningful and interesting by emphasizing real-world problem solving and self-discovery of mathematical theory and concepts. Therein lies the criticism of this program—many parents feel that the students don't learn basic skills, that teachers are no longer a part of the process, and that the discovery learning approach translates into students teaching themselves. They feel that the new-new math has very little to do with math. Critics contend that the exercises are too focused on feelings or self-esteem and rely too much on group work and calculators (Price, 1999). Proponents are quick to cite improved test scores as evidence of the Everyday Math program's effectiveness. Anecdotal reports from school districts indicated that Everyday Math students did as well in computation sections of standardized tests, and much better in problem solving than traditional students (Carroll, 1993).

Grade Levels   K through 12

Materials Needed   An Everyday Math Kit for teachers is required. It contains:

- Manuals A and B
- Reference book (How to Play Math Games)

- Homelink (letters to parents on changes in areas of study)
- Sample of student workbooks
- Skillink (to give students additional practice beyond application)
- Resource book (student handout masters)
- Sunrise/Sunset chart for graphing (optional)
- Weather chart to chart weather differences (optional)

Student supplies include two consumable workbooks, one deck of cards, and a toolkit made by teachers (materials such as tape measures, clocks, thermometers, and money are put in the kit a day or two before the lesson).

Barriers to Implementation   Cost can be a factor that impedes implementation, particularly when the entire district does not adopt the program and the individual school has to fund the project.

Status   Overall, the Everyday Math program gets positive reviews from teachers. A major criticism is the substantial amount of preparation time involved in effectively implementing the program.

Training and Resources   The company offers 2- to 3-day workshops for teachers. They also provide teachers with a newsletter that addresses current concerns and offers suggestions for practice.

Concerns

I am afraid that the minimal drill skills will have a negative effect on my students' performance on standardized tests. (Teacher of the Year, Illinois)

Although I disagree, I've heard many teachers in the district complain that the program is not teacher-friendly, that you can't just open the book, that the directions are there and it's easy to follow. (Teacher of the Year, Texas)

Benefits

I teach at-risk second-graders, who were somewhat apathetic about math. Now that I'm using this program, my students are excited about math; they actually look forward to math time. There is a lot of up-front preparation involved, but I think my kids are worth it. (Teacher of the Year, Texas)

Rigorous and spiraled. (Teacher of the Year, Idaho)

I am amazed that students that are successful math students from prestigious suburbs have improved as a result of this program. (Teacher of the Year, New Jersey)

Reflections   This program is well grounded in theory. It embraces Dewey's (1938) classic philosophy of experiential learning, which is modernized by Bruner's (1961) discovery learning. Children learn by doing, which gives positive marks to the hands-on approach used by this program. The curriculum encourages a constructivist (Moshman, 1982) approach to learning by inviting students to construct their own meaning from mathematical theory and concepts. The use of a spiral-type curriculum is supported by information processing theory (Schunk, 1996) and brain-based learning principles (Sousa, 1998). The program focuses on real-world problem solving, which fosters authentic instruction and authentic assessment (Darling-Hammond, 1991). The focus on problem solving is further supported by Bloom's (1956) advocacy of higher-order thinking skills in his taxonomy of instructional objectives. To be effective, I think this program would require that teachers function as very astute facilitators, knowing when to let children work on their own and knowing when to step in and teach a concept, such as Vygotsky (1987) proposes in his notion of a zone of proximal development. As with any program, the teachers should not abandon their roles as teachers; they should frequently assess the effectiveness of the program and be ready to supplement it with traditional forms of instruction if necessary. Teachers should be cautioned that over-reliance on calculators can rob students of the fundamentals of mathematical process that are necessary for them to solve problems on their own.

Creative Education Institute (CEI) Reading Program

The Creative Education Institute (CEI) is dedicated to researching and designing programs to help people improve their reading and math skills. CEI was established in 1987. Like many other programs, it subscribes to the premise that everyone can learn given the appropriate conditions and opportunities. The goal of the CEI program is to help students who have learning difficulties to build their language skills. Specific exercises in the CEI program are structured to develop new learning patterns, and to diminish and then strengthen weak areas of processing information. The foundation of the program is based on brain theory and on the brain's ability to develop new pathways for learning. This brain-retraining approach to remediation is touted as therapeutic because it effectively helps students find their paths to learning.

Materials and Procedures   The CEI program is an interactive, computer-based approach to addressing learning differences and difficulties such as auditory and visual problems, poor eye movement coordination, and sensory integration problems. To improve students' cognitive processing abilities, the program uses a prescriptive series of sensory-integrated exercises that attempts to link visual, auditory, and motor kinesthetic pathways in the brain. The program targets anyone having reading difficulties, including dyslexic students, special education students, at-risk, Title I, ESL/Bilingual adults, and underachieving or low-performing students.

CEI developed Essential Learning Systems (ELS; Creative Education Institute, 1997) a software program designed to address the causes rather than the symptoms of reading difficulties. ELS is based on multisensory learning, which employs all the senses in the reception and processing of information. ELS functions as a system, using generated speech (auditory), screen images (visual), and keyboarding (motor-kinesthetic), which distinguishes it from other remedial learning programs. Materials include assessment tests, such as the Learning Efficiency Test II to ascertain each student's level of processing efficiency and the Diagnostic Screening Tests for reading, that provide a grade-equivalency baseline. The ELS Placement Test determines the appropriate level and lesson (CEI, 2000a).

The CEI Reading Program is usually conducted in a laboratory setting using computer stations, the ELS software, and a lab facilitator complete with technical support. CEI consultants visit the school frequently to provide needed support. The lab facilitator is trained and hired to run the lab. Dell Computer entered into a partnership with CEI to provide computers with preloaded CEI programs that would be shipped directly to the schools (CEI, 2000b). Students in the ELS program receive direct instruction in addition to computer-assisted instruction. They are taught to understand how sounds are connected to the written word. Their reading fluency is further enhanced as they are presented with words of varying difficulty, until they have gained automaticity. Computer-assisted instruction encourages automaticity and fosters mastery. Increased speed usually signals automaticity. The computer is useful for monitoring and checking student progress and for providing immediate feedback and progress reports. Headphones are used at each workstation to enhance cognitive functioning by helping the student stay focused and to avoid distracting environmental stimuli.

Barriers to Implementation   There are no apparent barriers, other than the cost of the computer hardware. It seems that schools would need adequate space to set up CEI learning labs. Poor technical support could significantly affect the program. I think having a consultant frequently visit and service the program is very proactive, particularly for a program that relies heavily on technology.

Status   Most references to the CEI program have been positive. Evaluation results and comments from program users are available on the CEI Web site. The results attribute significant gains to the CEI program. One school district reported average gains of 2 to 3 years in grade equivalency scores. Supporters of CEI contend that it also raises students' self-esteem and classroom performance. The program is relatively new, so very little information about it is available in the literature. According to the Creative Education Institute, over 3 million students in at least 5 million schools have used the CEI programs.

Reflections   The therapeutic, holistic approach used by CEI is timely and well grounded in theory. CEI is primarily a cognitive model based on the information processing theory that subscribes to the multistore theory of sensory memory, short-term memory, and long-term memory (Schunk, 2000). Using the computer to link auditory, visual, motor-kinesthetic tasks to build and strengthen neural pathways provides the timely added dimension of experiential, multisensory teaching that is very similar to the Orton-Gillingham approach (Orton-Gillingham Academy, 1998). The CEI program is on the cutting edge of research, implementing the latest in technology and brain-based learning. The CEI program is a bold venture with a promising future.

Drug Abuse Resistance Education (D.A.R.E.)

The nationwide, school-based Drug Abuse Resistance Education program, popularly referred to as D.A.R.E., is a substance abuse prevention program that targets young children. It uses trained, uniformed law enforcement officers to teach children how to resist drugs by teaching them to never start using them. The law officers stress the importance of resisting peer pressure to start using drugs. Using role-play and other strategies, the officers help students develop effective ways of refusing alcohol and drugs. Special attention is given to bolstering student self-esteem and self-confidence to decrease their vulnerability to peer pressure.

The D.A.R.E. program was created in 1983 as a joint project between the Los Angeles Unified School District and the Los Angeles Police Department (U.S. Department of Justice, 1994). The D.A.R.E. motto is "DARE to keep children off drugs." The purpose of D.A.R.E. is to educate children who are attending school and who are not necessarily involved in drugs. The focus is on preventive intervention rather than the type of intervention used with active drug and alcohol users. D.A.R.E. America is a California-based corporation that manages the program and the merchandise. The 25-person board of directors features several Hollywood celebrities. Funding comes from private donations, tax revenue, and royalties from sales of D.A.R.E. merchandise.

Grade Levels The D.A.R.E. program is designed specifically for grades K–12, but it is usually taught in the fifth grade. The program features a 17-week curriculum complete with workbooks containing 17 hour-long weekly lessons that: (1) introduce D.A.R.E.; (2) look at the effects of mind-altering drugs; (3) consider the consequences of drug use; (4) examine changing beliefs about drug use; (5) identify resistance techniques or ways to say no; (6) look at building self-esteem; (7) teach assertiveness; (8) identify ways to manage stress without taking drugs; (9) offer strategies for reducing violence; (10) give techniques for combating media influences on drug use and violence; (11) consider how to make decisions about risky behavior; (12) encourage saying yes to positive alternatives; (13) encourage having positive role models; (14) look at ways to resist gang and group violence; (15) summarize D.A.R.E. lessons; (16) encourage taking a stand; and (17) provide a D.A.R.E. culmination. As part of the culmination, program participants sign pledges to keep their bodies free of alcohol, tobacco, and drugs. They have a ceremony during which they sing songs and are presented with pins, T-shirts, identification cards, and certificates.

D.A.R.E. officers receive about 80 hours of professional training in areas such as child development, instructional strategies, and classroom management. These law officers go into the schools to teach the lessons on a weekly basis.

Barriers to Implementation   Two clearly recognizable barriers would be funding and the allocation of adequate time. Hansen and McNeal (1997) reported that D.A.R.E. program costs were about $750 million. A lack of adequate funding to provide enough law officers for all schools that want a D.A.R.E. program would be a barrier for some schools. In addition, because D.A.R.E. and other external programs must compete for precious allocated instructional time, a lack of adequate instructional time could be a barrier. Such programs may meet with some teacher resistance when teachers need the time for their lessons. Most teachers are cooperative, but guard their time more when standardized tests are scheduled.

Benefits   The D.A.R.E. program is proactive; it exposes children to the dangers of drugs and teaches them how to resist efforts to get involved with drugs.

> *This has to work—the alternative is to give up—unthinkable. (Teacher of the Year, New Jersey)*

> *Makes community and students aware of drugs and consequences. (Teacher of the Year, Hawaii)*

> *Kids are aware! Not all parents are, however, and not all teachers are aware of the signals of drug use in their students. Maybe students could share or teach the school personnel, helping us to know how to help them avoid the traps of addiction. (Teacher of the Year, Oregon)*

Concerns   A major concern is whether D.A.R.E. can demonstrate research-based proof of effectiveness that supports claims of reductions in the onset and use of drugs, alcohol, and tobacco in children. Some programs have been discontinued or have lost funding because of an inability to show the level of effectiveness that would warrant continuation (Janofsky, 2000). Research-based reviews of the effectiveness of D.A.R.E. offer mixed opinions. Some say the program is very effective (Ringwalt, Green, Ennett, Iachan, Clayton, & Lukefeld, 1994; Landry, 1998). Others conclude that the program was ineffective, and there was no significant reduction in self-reported alcohol and drug use (Lynam et al., 1999).

The curriculum is a matter of some concern to the Drug Reform Coordination Network (DRCNet) because it does not undergo review by educators and administrators. A study conducted by the Research Triangle Institute (Chapel Hill Herald, 1993) confirmed the popularity of D.A.R.E but suggested that the program has a limited effect on drug use and could benefit from more interactive strategies and more emphasis on social and general competencies.

> *We make sure we teach this yearly, often at the expense of other health issues we should address. (Teacher of the Year, Idaho)*

*Programs are limited by law and social permissiveness. The program
needs to be instituted on a societal basis rather than as school child
problem. (Teacher of the Year, Montana)*

Reflections   A major underlying assumption of the D.A.R.E program is
the power of social learning, influence, and pressure on young children.
The underlying fear is that children in fifth and sixth grade are approach-
ing an age of experimentation when they are very vulnerable and sus-
ceptible to peer pressure, adult influence, and curiosity. Bandura's (1986)
work with social learning and triadic reciprocity, in particular, shows that
a person's environment and the behavior of others can have a powerful
effect on that person.

I think the D.A.R.E. curriculum reflects the importance of social influence and seeks to minimize the effects by strengthening a child's self-
esteem and confidence, thus giving the child the resources to be assertive
when approached with invitations or suggestions to experiment with
drugs. Recognizing the power of social influence is very relevant for poor
children, who according to Maslow (1970) must strive to satisfy their deficiency needs of survival, safety, self-esteem, and the need to belong. The
lures of using drugs, getting money from selling drugs, and being involved
in gang activity are especially seductive avenues for satisfying deficiency
needs. A program such as D.A.R.E. gives children the much-needed personal strength and knowledge to resist peer pressure as well as the environmental and economic pressures to experiment with alcohol, tobacco,
and other drugs.

Edison Project/Edison Schools

In 1991, Steven Whittle announced that he would create a new kind of
school—a school that would provide the best education in the world for all
students. Whittle believed that all students could learn if given an exciting,
meaningful curriculum, adequate learning time, and adequate technology.
His new school would serve all students, the low achievers as well as high
achievers. The Edison Project is a schoolwide reform model that uses a partnership school format. Partnership schools work jointly with the school system, parents, and the community to meet academic goals.

Whittle had initially proposed to raise $2 billion to start 1,000 schools.
In the wake of the declining popularity of school vouchers, that plan was
abandoned. The Edison Project instead opted to focus on managing public
schools. The Edison Project is a for-profit company. The original plan was
for the Edison Project to assume responsibility by managing the education
program, the needed technology, and the day-to-day school operations in
exchange for the money that is allocated per pupil for instruction. The company also would receive all monies for Title I, special education, operating
expenditures, and so on.

Whittle teamed up with Bruno Schmidt. They renamed the Edison Project, changing it to Edison Schools. Edison schools are organized into houses of 110 to 120 multiage students. Four to six teachers are usually assigned to each house. Students stay with their respective houses for 2 or 3 years.

Grade Levels   Each school may be divided into as many as six houses or academies:

- Readiness (pre-K)
- Primary (K–2)
- Elementary (3–5)
- Junior (6–8)
- Senior (9–10)
- Collegiate (11–12)

Materials and Procedures   The program features an extended school day and school year, to give students more opportunity for learning. Each student is provided with a computer to facilitate home-school relations and communication and to give students access to current technology. Added benefits are the extended use of the school as a community center and the availability of a community resource director to provide any necessary social services.

Barriers to Implementation   School administrators are usually selected because they share the philosophy of the project. On the other hand, high teacher turnover suggests that some teachers may resist the Edison concept. Ladd (2000) reports that at one school, about 27 percent of the teachers left by the first year. Of course, some of that departure is probably due to normal matriculation. Increased faculty turnover may also be attributed to Edison's heavy reliance on inexperienced teachers. Another barrier is parent resistance to participation. Parent participation is a critical part of the Edison Schools project.

Concerns   A major concern is the scheduling logistics for students making transitions from one class to another (Garcia, 1995). Classes are much larger than promised. Consequently, high enrollments, coupled with the program's heavy reliance on technology, often translate into computer shortages. Teachers may not receive adequate training time for the programs they are supposed to teach (Garcia, 1995). Sometimes parents and students lack the necessary computer literacy to participate in the technology component of the program. There may also be time delays while trying to bring them on board.

Status   Despite its problems and limitations, the program offers a good curriculum and an excellent technology component. The Edison Project is currently serving over 50 schools, and many schools have long waiting lists (1,600 at one school). Student achievement is up; kindergartners and first-graders in Edison Schools appear to have stronger reading skills than their counterparts in other schools. Some students have increased their test scores over 25 percentiles. In a recent survey, 90 percent of parents rated the school as A or B. Almost 75 percent of students gave the school an A or B rating.

The expected success outcomes for the Edison Schools were high. Whether the project lived up to those expectations depends on who is asked. Reviews are mixed—the company and some respondents say yes; others disagree.

Reflections　At first glance the Edison Schools program seems wonderful. However, its experimental nature is troublesome. Children who are already deemed at-risk can least afford being associated with an academic experiment that could go awry. Some staff development training on working with at-risk children might offset some of that risk. Farber's (1998) article illuminates the gravity and severity of lacking knowledge of how to work with at-risk, inner-city children. Farber acknowledges that although these children may have more to lose if the experiment goes bad, they also have a lot to gain if all goes well.

Effective Schools

James Coleman wrote a controversial paper alleging that children could not learn if they were from poor homes that did not have the proper conditions and values to support education. His research concluded that the school's role was insignificant; poor children could not achieve, no matter what the school did. Coleman's paper caused a furor among educators and researchers, who believed his results were suspect. The study seized the attention of Ronald Edmonds (1979a, 1979b), who adamantly resisted the absoluteness of Coleman's claim. Edmonds launched his own research study, with the goals of finding schools where poor children were achieving and ascertaining why poor children were learning in certain schools and not in others. Edmonds conducted comparative research on both types of schools and found that poor children could learn in public schools. His research provided significant evidence that all children could learn, given the proper conditions for learning. The research revealed seven correlates or characteristics of effective schools (Association for Effective Schools, 2000):

1. A Clear School Mission—Everyone involved with the educational process helps to develop a clearly articulated, well-focused mission statement. All involved must be committed to the goals, priorities, objectives, and responsibilities to ensure success.
2. High Expectations for Success—The school has a climate of high expectations for all students; educators believe that all students can learn.

3. Instructional Leadership—Administrators are leaders who work cooperatively with teachers and staff to apply the characteristics of instructional effectiveness.
4. Frequent Monitoring of Student Progress—Use assessment procedures to improve the performance of all students.
5. Opportunity to Learn and Student Time on Task—Teachers maximize the engaged time that students spend on task, using proven instructional techniques.
6. Safe and Orderly Environment—The effective school provides a safe, businesslike environment that is free from any threats of violence or physical harm.
7. Positive Home-School Relations—Parents are committed to supporting the school and its mission statement. Lezotte's (1995) research verifies that these correlates continue to accurately describe effective schools.

Research on these correlates has spanned more than 25 years. Replication research and cross-validation studies have resulted in a second generation of correlates that are an enhanced, enlightened version of the first seven.

Grade Levels   Pre-K through 12

Materials   Using the effective schools research strategies, Effective Schools Inc. offers a variety of videos and written material to help schools implement systemic change. Currently, a video and a book on the total-quality effective school are available for a moderate sum (under $500). Books on the process are relatively inexpensive. To purchase all available products could cost several thousand dollars. Consulting and online services are available.

Barriers to Implementation   Time is truly a barrier to implementation of the effective schools process. Teachers must buy into the belief that collaboration, although costly in terms of time, is necessary for schools to be effective.

Status   Effective Schools is now a schoolwide improvement process, based on effective schools research that embraces the notion that all children can learn. Many schools across the nation are using this process or program at all grade levels. It has a high level of success.

Benefits

A must if our nation is to survive. (Teacher of the Year, New Jersey)

It's a part of our Management of Change. (Teacher of the Year, Idaho)

Community-building is always a good idea. Effective schools programs help to identify the strong elements in a school, and help to enlist community support for programs. (Teacher of the Year, Oregon)

Concerns

This has taken a lot of our district's focus the last three years. (Teacher of the Year, Idaho)

It takes a strong leader to keep it moving forward, and not let it become just an interesting exercise. (Teacher of the Year, Oregon)

Reflections The effective schools concept was bound to have some measure of success because it was a counter to the questionable claim made by Coleman in his report for the U.S. Office of Education that poor children cannot learn, regardless of what schools do. Such a blanket generalization has virtually zero probability of being true.

Research has shown that truly resilient children can thrive and achieve in the worst conditions, including impoverished, disenfranchised families. Studies such as the one by Turner, Norman, and Zuny (1995) offer discussion of envirosocial versus innate behaviors as an explanation of resiliency. Why children are resilient is still a source of controversy and debate, but the "what"—the correlates of student success identified in effective schools research—has provided a blueprint for success. Levine and Levine (1999) refer to the correlates as prerequisites for success. I think they work because they diminish the adverse effects of the poor children's environment.

Emergent Literacy

Marie Clay (1966), a New Zealand researcher, introduced the term emergent literacy to describe the abilities, experience, exposures, interests, and reading and writing behaviors that occur early in a child's life that foster the development of conventional literacy. These behaviors include but are not limited to using pictures and context to "read" stories, imitating reading by acting as if they are reading, trying to write, making up a story using a book and "reading" it orally. Such pre-reading activities may manifest long before a child enters school. Acknowledgment and support from adults will help to sustain the child's emerging literacy skills.

Researchers such as Teale (1986) believe that "reading readiness" inadequately describes the process that takes place as a child starts to read and write, because it suggests there is a specific time when this "reading" occurs. Instead, these researchers believe the ability to read and write is an innate trait that emerges over time.

Researchers observing young children have identified a variety of preliteracy indicators—classified as literacy events, literacy behaviors, conditions of literacy, and literacy development. They have conducted studies in the homes of early readers to ascertain characteristics that may be favorable for developing literacy.

The Emergent Literacy Project (University of Idaho, 1999) examined current research and identified six elements of emerging literacy:

1. Children learn to read and write early in life.
2. Learning to read and write develops concurrently, as opposed to the notion that children must read before they can write.
3. Literacy should be functional and authentic, fully associated with real life.
4. Children learn literacy by doing or being actively engaged.
5. Reading to a child is a major contribution to the child's literacy development.
6. Learning to read and write is a developmental process that is influenced by age, environment, and opportunity.

Emergent literacy is taught through singing songs, reading books, rhyming, talking, questioning, writing stories, telling stories, playing games, and so on. Parents can begin literacy activities in early infancy by playing songs and reading to a child. Activities should be developmentally appropriate for each child. The Early Success Program is an emergent literacy program that stresses phonemic awareness or knowledge of the letters and sounds in words in addition to reading and writing.

Grade Levels   Pre-K through K

Materials   The Early Success Program is available in a kit for about $1,000. Only one kit per classroom is needed. Each kit contains lesson plans, stories summaries, evaluation forms, cards for word play, and so forth. A bilingual version is also available. The home school component makes it easy for parents to use. The program is organized into 30 weekly programs. Children focus on one story each week and actively engage in reading the story and writing about it. They take story summaries home for added practice.

Barriers to Implementation   A major barrier is lack of exposure to literacy activities and materials early in life. Social class may be a barrier to emergent literacy. Whitehurst (1999) points out that children from low socioeconomic backgrounds may have fewer opportunities to interact with books, fewer parent-child reading interactions, fewer literacy resources, and less than optimal linguistic opportunities at home and in school. Clay (1966) believes that children from cultures that rely heavily on oral language and less on written may encounter problems with emergent literacy. A barrier to implementation in schools is low parent participation (Neuman, 2000).

Low literacy rates of parents may be a major factor in parents' resistance to participating in emergent literacy activities.

Status   Emergent literacy programs make an important contribution to the literacy development of children. The success of these programs is readily observed in the number of students who become successful readers at an earlier age. Students who are not exposed to emergent activities appear to struggle more while learning to read and may take longer to learn to read.

Benefits   Children may learn to read and write long before they begin formal schooling. The concept of emergent literacy calls for reassessing the concept of reading readiness and its role in literacy. Schools that adopt emergent literacy programs in kindergarten, pre-K, and primary grades increase the odds of having good readers by third grade.

Allows children to make incremental steps in learning to read. (Teacher of the Year, Idaho)

Children can feel successful early on in the educational process. (Teacher of the Year, Idaho)

Concerns   The Emergent Literacy Project (University of Idaho, 1999) supported students in reconstructing the meaning of a book as they attempt to reread it, and in reconstructing their written language skills, resulting in activities such as invented spelling (where students spell words in a phonetic way that makes sense to them). Invented spelling demonstrates phonemic awareness, but it does not take into consideration the difficulties of unlearning.

Reflections   Literacy development may be likened to cognitive development (Piaget, 1970) in that both are thought to develop in stages, over time, with limitations. Learning to read and learning to write involve developmental processes that also occur in stages (Mason, 1980; Sulzby, Barnhart, & Hiesima, 1990). Some advocates of emergent literacy see children's reading and writing limitations, such as invented spelling and invented stories using picture cues, from a constructivist point of view. They believe that children are constructing their own meanings from books and from written words, so it's acceptable to have misspelled words and stories that don't relate to the actual story in the book. Acceptance of invented spellings and stories are fine, as long as the child continues to progress through the development process and successfully acquires conventional expressions of literacy. Adult support and assistance in the children's zone of proximal development (Vygotsky, 1987) can help them engage in emergent literacy activities and make the leap to conventional literacy. It is not in children's best interest to let them languish in the stage of invented spellings and picture-cued stories and be viewed as deficient because they have not developed the expected, requisite skills for literacy.

Expeditionary Learning Outward Bound (ELOB)

The Outward Bound program was founded by Kurt Hahn in 1941. The Outward Bound program developed the Expeditionary Learning Outward Bound (ELOB) program in 1992 using the same principles created by Hahn for Outward Bound. Expeditionary learning is a teaching reform model that advocates extending teaching beyond the boundaries of the traditional classroom. It is a type of learning in which teachers use the scaffolding approach to guide students on a learning expedition into the unknown, encouraging self-discovery while helping students to construct knowledge. Its premise is that people discover their capabilities when faced with challenges and the unexpected. Expeditionary Learning is intended to enhance teaching by using self-discovery, meaningfulness, and context to study a topic in depth. Teachers encourage mutual trust and respect through cooperative, collaborative efforts. Competing with oneself to achieve personal standards of excellence is the preferred method of competition.

Grade Levels K through 12

Components Expeditionary Learning is a schoolwide concept that embraces five core practices and 10 principles developed by Kurt Hahn. The five core practices are as follows:

1. Using learning expeditions during which students explore a topic in depth, going wherever their quest for information sends them. This practice often includes going outside of the classroom and gathering information in authentic settings
2. Allowing students plenty of time for reflection and critique
3. Promoting a school culture of achievement, high expectations, collaboration, and respect for diversity
4. Establishing a flexible school structure that accommodates long-term, project-based learning that often requires large blocks of time
5. Using school review as a tool to improve the quality of teaching and learning

The following are the 10 design principles of Expeditionary Learning:

1. Stressing the primacy of self-discovery
2. Encouraging the having of wonderful ideas
3. Accepting the responsibility for learning
4. Providing intimacy and caring
5. Making effective use of success and failure
6. Valuing collaboration and cooperation
7. Respecting diversity and inclusivity
8. Having respectful relationships with the natural world

9. Providing time for solitude and reflection
10. Preparing students for service and compassion

Barriers to Implementation One of the most significant barriers to implementation is most likely time. Implementing an ELOB program may require as much as 20 days of professional development per teacher, a 5-day institute for faculty, 2 days for initial setup, and 3 hours weekly dedicated to team planning. Resistance is a barrier. Proponents believe that at least 80 percent of the faculty must buy into the ELOB concept for it to be effective. Faculty members may resist the change required to implement an Expeditionary Learning program because it is radically different from traditional instruction.

Scheduling also poses a barrier to implementation. Expeditionary learning programs require a lot of flexibility, large blocks of allocated time for frequent expeditions, and time for student reflection.

Limitations Although ELOB is an excellent program, it probably shares some of the same limitations as discovery learning. Both require ample time for students to find a solution or to achieve a goal. The problem is that even with ample time, students may not ever find a solution or reach a goal.

Benefits The use of authentic projects and activities is a very appealing aspect of the ELOB program. The program attempts to serve all students, regardless of special needs, ethnicity, socioeconomic status, limited English status, and so on.

Status To date, approximately 47 schools are using ELOB programs. Student participants usually show improvement in test scores. Improvement varies by years of participation and by district. There may be some improvement by the first year; but by the third year, 9 out of 10 ELOB schools show improvement.

Reflections Expeditionary Learning Outward Bound programs appear to be exciting, learner-centered programs. I believe this program is distinguished by the integration of affect or feelings and emotion into the learning process. For example, central to the core beliefs of ELOB is the idea that learning occurs best when there is emotion (Vygotsky, 1987). The heavily constructivist approach to learning is commendable; as mentioned earlier, adults use a scaffolding approach to help students construct knowledge and to overcome their fear of discovery (Bruner, 1961). The program has a most worthy goal of helping students develop a passion for learning. I think it is noteworthy that ELOB programs recognize that a psychologically safe, nurturing educational environment is most conducive to learning.

Gifted and Talented

National attention has been focused on improving the skills and test scores of American students. In this context, however, little attention has been paid to the gifted and talented (GT) students. This oversight is counterproductive to our national mission to educate all students and encourage them to work up to their full potential. Lewis Terman (1925) coined the term gifted. Students who scored in the top 1 percent on the Stanford-Binet Intelligence Test or a comparable test were considered gifted. Definitions vary by state and school district, but overall, a gifted student is one who shows exemplary or exceptional abilities in one or more areas when compared to students of the same age, experience, and grade level.

The plight of gifted students first came to light when educators noticed that many of the gifted students were bored and apathetic about traditional schoolwork. Studies revealed that students recognized as gifted required challenges, activities, and services beyond the traditional classroom offerings. Programs for gifted students sprang up across the country with a goal of improving education, services, and curriculum for children with exceptional talents and abilities. The newly acquired recognition of gifted students created a new set of controversies and concerns.

Now, gifted students run the risk of being overlooked in the classroom. Many teachers have developed the mistaken impression that gifted students are super learners who do not need much help from the teacher, are expected to maintain a high level of performance, can acquire concepts rapidly, and have a high level of knowledge in all areas. This type of thinking influenced the development of many psychological consequences for gifted students. Feeling the pressures of the high expectations being imposed on them has increased the risk of GT students developing a need for perfectionism (Orange, 1997). In most cases, GT students are expected to maintain a high level of performance to remain in the GT program.

Grade Levels   Gifted and talented programs are found across all grade levels.

Training and Procedures   Gifted and talented programs vary from state to state on criteria, procedures, definitions, and so on. In most states, teachers receive special training to teach GT classes. Texas requires 60 hours of initial training and 6 hours annually for continued certification (Texas Association for the Gifted and Talented, 1996). Teachers usually nominate students to be tested for gifted and talent programs. Tests vary by state. States may use aptitude tests, achievement tests, ability tests, checklists, criteria, and so on. Usually a designated committee or individual makes the final selection. Most GT programs accelerate the curriculum in specialty areas such as math, science, or music. In the gifted and talented magnet schools, or in special schools for the gifted, the entire curriculum may be accelerated.

Funding   Program costs vary. Although some states allocate funds for GT programs, there is often a cap on the number of students who can participate. The school district usually contributes the bulk of the funding for teacher training, materials, books, workshops, and other resources.

Benefits   Research indicates that gifted and talented schools are very effective. Students are highly motivated. Students participating in the gifted and talented programs usually have high scores on achievement tests. Many become merit scholars, and very few drop out of school.

> *Students that are identified as gifted are given an opportunity to go above and beyond what is discussed in the classroom. (Teacher of the Year, Missouri)*

> *A great idea. (Teacher of the Year, New Jersey)*

> *Gifted & Talented Program: We have two elementary programs. One is a self-contained school for the gifted and talented. The other is to have those students clustered on a grade level in one teacher's class. She is trained in strategies that work well with these children. A gifted resource teacher comes in each day to co-teach. The key here is "co-teaching." The regular teacher learns strategies that work well with all children; the other kids in the room can take part. They blossom. Only problem is that this class is full of the high achievers. That may not leave many above-average kids to place in the other classes. But it seems to work well. I like this idea better than the self-contained school because those kids often have a long drive to get there and are not part of the neighborhood in a way. They are a bit isolated and outcast. Gifted kids feel different anyway. But when they get to middle school, we have a fabulous magnet program for gifted. They even partner up with the local med school and observe brain surgery, among other programs. The high schools have academies (interest, not giftedness) or magnets, like fine arts and technology for the gifted. (Teacher of the Year, Virginia)*

Concerns and Limitations   Reading, ability representation, and assessments are major limitations in terms of effectiveness. Student's reading ability may confound the selection process, resulting in erroneous selection or omission of students. Students who read well at an early age may be targeted as gifted and fail to meet the expectations for GT students later. On the other hand, students who are delayed in their reading ability may meet the GT criteria later. Under-representation of African American, Mexican American, and other group participation in gifted and talented programs is a grave concern. Low representation may be attributed to test bias (Cantu, 1998). Restricting selection assessment to only verbal instruments is problematic and may preclude the participation of some minority students.

> *A great idea as long as it doesn't breed elitism. (Teacher of the Year, New Jersey)*

> *We do a poor job of meeting the needs of gifted and talented kids. (Teacher of the Year, Idaho)*

By the time those students get to high school, they are indistinguishable from good students that did not have the opportunity. It is more of a desired social status for parents than it is an acceleration for students. (Teacher of the Year, Montana)

Reflections Howard Gardner's (1993) research on multiple intelligences strengthens the argument for the need to use alternative assessments in the selection for and continued participation in GT programs. Gardner's theory of multiple intelligences proposes that there are at least seven intelligences that involve logical mathematical, linguistic, bodily kinesthetic, musical, spatial, interpersonal skills, intrapersonal skills, and so on. Such intelligences cannot be adequately assessed using only a verbal instrument. The concept of multiple intelligences demands a variety of forms of nonverbal assessment. Using alternative assessment when needed may assure adequate and fair representation for all who qualify for a gifted and talented program—regardless of ethnicity, socioeconomic status, or culture.

Head Start

The Head Start program began as a combat strategy in President Lyndon Johnson's War on Poverty initiative. Johnson noticed that poor children were at risk of not being successful when they entered school, and that an appalling 50 percent of the nation's children were in poverty. He believed that education was the key to success for poor children and their only way out of the cycle of poverty (Styfco & Zigler, 2000). Dr. Robert Cooke formed a Head Start planning committee to develop an intervention with the purpose of giving poor children a "head start" so they would enter school with the same skills and abilities as their more affluent, advantaged peers and be more likely to experience success (Styfco & Zigler, 2000). The Office of Economic Opportunity established Head Start in 1965 as a child development summer program that lasted 6–8 weeks (Haynes, 2000). The program was committed to meeting the needs of young, at-risk children from low-income families. The program uses a comprehensive approach to fostering the socioemotional development, education, nutrition, and health of young children. It also provides social services for participating families.

Grade Levels The program targets preschool children ages 3–5 years.

Program Components Head Start is comprehensive in that it focuses on four areas that are important to child development:

- Provides a variety of learning experiences that facilitate the intellectual, social, and emotional development of poor children
- Provides critical health services such as immunizations, dental care, medical care, and so on

- Offers parent education, to take advantage of the parent as the first teacher and the one who carries on when the program ends
- Encourages parent involvement in all aspects of the program
- Assesses participating families to ascertain their needs and provide necessary social services

Barriers to Implementation   The government appropriates funds for Head Start programs. Public and private not-for-profit organizations are awarded grants for Head Start projects. A barrier to implementation might be that the community must contribute 20 percent of the total cost of a Head Start program. They may have difficulty raising the funds. The program also relies very heavily on volunteers and donations such as classroom space and materials from organizations.

Benefits   Since its inception in 1965, Head Start has effectively served over 15 million children and families. It has had a significant impact on the range and quality of services offered to poor children.

Concerns   Critics of the Head Start program express concern that segregation of poor children from others may be detrimental to the socialization and achievement of these children. Using IQ test gains as an evaluative measure of success is a source of concern. The IQ gains in the program were temporary. They showed evidence of fading in the first few years of school; consequently, the Head Start program lost credibility. A limitation was the lack of a clear, simple goal statement, which caused some people to focus on the cognitive aspect of the goal. Temporary IQ gains made it seem that the program did not meet its goals. This cognitive focus created a perception of Head Start as a cognitive enrichment program, when it was meant to be painted with a much broader brush. A main benefit of the program is the focus on child development.

> It is a program that substitutes parenting skills for another school responsibility, . . . and is viable because of the lack of parental responsibilities. (Teacher of the Year, Montana)

> Only 21% of eligible 3–4 year olds in Idaho attend. (Teacher of the Year, Idaho)

Reflections   Head Start's comprehensive, holistic approach to helping poor children is very humanistic and appropriate. Maslow (1970) made educators aware of the importance of satisfying basic needs in children before attempting higher-order needs. The Head Start program addresses many aspects of a child's life, in particular the basic needs. Having satisfied those needs, the constructivist approach to the curriculum offers a higher probability of success with young children. The use of developmentally appropriate instruction in Head Start will facilitate the transition to similar instruction as the child enters school, thereby meeting the overall goal of the Head Start program—to increase the academic readiness of poor children.

Health Occupations Students of America (HOSA)

Health Occupations Students of America (HOSA) is a national Career and Technical Student Organization (CTSO) endorsed by the Department of Education and the Health Occupations Education Division of the American Vocational Association. HOSA is an exclusive program restricted to secondary students, college students, and adults who are enrolled in health occupations classes. Secondary Health Occupations Education (HOE) educates students enrolled in vocational, technical, and comprehensive programs. The HOSA organization was founded in 1976. It has grown to over 60,000 members through 34 affiliated states and involvement in 4 unaffiliated state associations featuring 2,200 chapters to date (Health Occupations Students of America (HOSA), 1999). HOSA has a dual mission of promoting career opportunities in health care and enhancing the quality of health care. Its purpose is not only to provide opportunities for health-care students to increase their knowledge and leadership skills but also to address the problem of an acute shortage of qualified workers in the health-care industry.

Materials and Procedures   HOSA is integral part of the Health Science Technology curriculum. It is usually a vocational class that offers students hands-on training and observation. HOSA educates students in approved health-care programs in vocational, technical, and comprehensive high schools. Students enrolled in HOSA classes are assigned to nearby hospitals for their training. HOSA features a self-paced, individualized program open to all HOSA members. There are four levels of increasing difficulty: first level (Helper), second level (Organizer), third level (Specialist), and fourth level (Achiever). Members who complete all four levels receive national recognition at the HOSA National Leadership Conference. Students who are HOSA members wear a white tailored shirt or blouse, navy blue blazer with the emblem placed over the heart, and white slacks.

Benefits   The benefits of the HOSA program are obvious. It gives students realistic expectations of their career choices and a better understanding of health-related issues. It raises students' self-esteem and heightens their motivation.

Reflections   I am impressed with HOSA's efforts to instill a sense of community and belonging in its students. I think having a mission statement, a motto, a creed, and official colors and dress conveys the serious nature of the project. I think the HOSA focus on self-competition and self-paced, individualized opportunities for recognition are timely and theoretically grounded. HOSA appears to be an effective way to address the shortage of health-care workers. Helping students get a preview of what's to come increases the likelihood that those who stay will be committed to their profession, compassionate in their delivery of service, and skillful in their efforts to help people.

Jumpstart

Jumpstart is a mentoring project, started by two students from Yale University who attended a summer camp in 1993. While working with preschoolers, the students had an experience that was so positive that it inspired in them a vision of universities working with young children to promote literacy and to circumvent school failure and underachievement. This vision became the wellspring of the Jumpstart program, which would provide intervention at the earliest strategic point—preschool.

The two students believed that universities had the resources and people power to really make a difference in the lives of preschoolers. The Jumpstart program recruits college students from AmeriCorps, a volunteer organization. These student volunteers are paired with preschoolers who appear to be having difficulty in an early childhood education program such as Head Start (Jumpstart, 2000).

The AmeriCorps volunteers are trained using the High/Scope approach to teaching preschoolers readiness skills. This approach was developed by the High/Scope Educational Research Foundation, a nonprofit organization specializing in research, curriculum development, and training professionals.

Children participating in the program are usually referred by a teacher who suspects that a child is having difficulty. Teachers consult a checklist of social skills, literacy, and language development to ascertain a child's candidacy for the Jumpstart program. The college students and the children are paired to work together one-on-one in a 20-month-long mentoring session. Participating college students receive free tuition as compensation for their services.

Originators of Jumpstart identified a threefold purpose of the program: (1) to build on children's successes, (2) to encourage family involvement, and (3) to prepare future teachers to build on students' success. The program is guided by 17 success outcomes in the areas of language, literacy, and social relations. Parents are encouraged to fulfill their role as their child's first teacher. Every effort is made to bring home and school together. AmeriCorps volunteers gain valuable experience that will transfer into their classrooms when they become teachers. As teachers, they will become invaluable assets in recognizing student problems and providing adequate intervention and remediation [Jumpstart University Start-Up Kit (Jumpstart, 2000)].

Grade Levels   Preschool

Barriers to Implementation   Cost may impede requests for university affiliation with Jumpstart. The cost for a Jumpstart program is prohibitive at $200,000 for start-up. The bulk of the cost is to pay for student workers. Approximately 10 percent goes to defray the cost of employing a site manager and doing the start-up. Couple the cost problems with those of conducting an intricate, multipurpose, multifaceted program and therein lies an effective barrier to the implementation of this very useful program.

Status   Despite its limitations, and resistance from those who don't believe that early intervention makes a significant difference, Jumpstart appears to be very successful. This success has fueled the expansion of the program from coast to coast.

Benefits   Jumpstart has been credited with some evidence of success. In 1999, 34 percent of Jumpstart participants (compared to 19 percent of non-participants) moved from below average to above average in language and literacy skills. In measures of literacy, language, and socialization skills, 32 percent of Jumpstart children (compared to 25 percent of the non-participants) moved from below average to above average (Jumpstart, 2000, p. 1).

> *Our kindergarten teachers work for free to provide this Jumpstart opportunity for our kindergarteners. We run it for 6 days prior to the start of the school. Parents come with their children. Preliminary assessments are done at that time. (Teacher of the Year, Idaho)*

Reflections   I attribute much of the success of this program to its use of experiential learning and social learning theory (Bandura, 1977; Dewey, 1938). These learning theories are consistent with the philosophy of the High/Scope Educational Research foundation, which contends that children who actively interact with academic tasks and other people have a tendency to learn more and to have better retention. The one-on-one mentoring process is ideal for making use of a child's zone of proximal development, or the point at which a child can master a challenging task if they receive appropriate assistance from a knowledgeable adult (Wertsch, 1991). The Jumpstart program has particular merit in that it targets such a critical time in children's lives—preschool. The preschool years are a time of rapid acquisition of information; the Jumpstart program could only enhance this process.

Modern Red Schoolhouse (MRSh)

The Modern Red Schoolhouse (MRSh) is a comprehensive reform model that takes the best features of character education and the rigor of the little red schoolhouse of the past and integrates them into a very modern concept of education. This program was developed by the Hudson Institute in 1992 and sponsored by the New American Schools, a nonprofit organization in Virginia. The Modern Red Schoolhouse modernizes the virtues and educational principles of old by embodying them with high expectations for achievement and infusing them with a good measure of technology and current information. The MRSh program is further defined by its goals of having all students aspire to and attain high levels of achievement. It works with all schools in five key areas: finance, technology, community involvement, curriculum, standards, and assignments. Committees are organized around planning restructuring efforts in all of these areas. The Modern Red Schoolhouse is recognized for its high academic standards. The basic principle of the MRSh is that students can reach high standards, and the program does not settle for less. It insists on mastery.

Although MRSh is fairly traditional in its approach and design, the pedagogy is modernized by considering students' learning styles, pacing and individual instructional needs, and innovative teaching methods. It features a standards-driven curriculum, professional development programs, alternative and traditional assessments, and community involvement efforts.

Grade Levels K through 12, featuring three divisions: primary, middle, and upper

Materials and Procedures The objectives of the Modern Red Schoolhouse are that students master a rigorous curriculum and meet standards high enough to prepare them to take advanced placement courses. Another objective is to foster the development of character. Students are frequently tracked and monitored for continuing progress using the Individual Education Compact, an agreement between teachers, students, and parents. This agreement features measurable goals and delineates parent and teacher responsibilities for improving student achievement. Individual Education Compacts are managed using technology (see the "Materials" description).

The MRSh program has benchmarked advanced placement exams in most subjects, and established standards for grade levels 4, 8, and 12. Students move through divisions in the Modern Red Schoolhouse. Advancement to the next division is contingent on passing watershed assessments of content, delivered in a variety of assessment formats such as oral exams, multiple-choice tests, and so on. Promotion is based on accumulating Hudson units, which are evidence of mastery of skills and knowledge.

Materials   Substantial, highly sophisticated technology is necessary for the MRSh program. Complete data, voice, and video systems must be a functional part of the Modern Red Schoolhouse design. The technology is multimedia; it features hard-wired teacher and student computer workstations, various software such as graphing programs, and an electronic encyclopedia. Electronic mail and voice delivery systems are also a part of the design.

The MRSh program uses two curriculums, E. D. Hirsch's Core Curriculum and the James Madison Series. A variety of standardized tests and the Individual Education Compact (essentially a contract or agreement to perform well) are essential to assessment, achievement, and placement. The organization also offers a variety of publications for parents, students, and educators.

Barriers to Implementation   The magnitude and breadth of the program command considerable time and resources. MRSh also requires substantial investment in highly sophisticated technology. Some school districts may not be equipped with the necessary hardware and software to accommodate the program. It is a labor-intensive, time-consuming effort. The initial implementation phase takes from 3 to 5 years, depending on the equipment and materials already available. Staff development, a critical element of the design, requires about 20 days per faculty member, with ongoing development beyond the initial phase (Modern Red Schoolhouse, 2000). Such a heavy time commitment may deter some teachers and negatively affect the program, because implementation is contingent upon 80 percent of the teachers agreeing to adopt the design. This contingency seems arbitrary and stringent; a 75 percent buy-in, along with a little program customization, might be equally effective.

Benefits   The Modern Red Schoolhouse program is currently being used in several states. Self-reports from participating teachers indicate that the program has had a significant positive impact on student achievement. Test results have increased in reading, writing, and math.

Concerns and Limitations   Schools may be limited in their pre-existing technology. Technology is critical to program success. For budgetary reasons, schools must often stagger the purchases of new equipment. A concern would be what is the impact on program effectiveness when a school does not have all the necessary equipment in place? Developing the Modern Red Schoolhouse infrastructure usually involves a construction and installation phase of wiring the building, preparing it for subsequent purchases of computers, telephones, cable TVs, and workstations. Ideally, the building would be ready for additional equipment, budget permitting. If the budget does not permit buying equipment, there is the sunken cost of preparing the building and the unfulfilled promise of a technology-driven program.

Reflections   I have visited schools that were wired for some type of technology that never materialized. These schools were not necessarily using

Modern Red Schoolhouse, but the various projects were in different stages of partial completion. Additional benefits of Modern Red Schoolhouse are most apparent in its concept of bringing the best practices from the past and enhancing and updating the content and delivery of those best practices using current technology. Combining the past with technology creates a sort of educational epoxy—like the glue, the strength is realized in the combination of the two parts. The best practices of the past serve to provide the rigor and pedagogy necessary to achieve mastery of the instructional content. The technology provides sensory enhancement that is very attractive and motivational to students.

National School Lunch Program (NSLP)

The National School Lunch Program (NSLP) is a federally assisted meal program that offers free or reduced-price lunches to low-income children across the nation. The program serves about 100,000 schools and feeds about 30 million children daily. Feeding school children began in the United States as sporadic, philanthropic efforts of organizations concerned with the needs of children. An official program was instituted by President Harry Truman's signing of the National School Lunch Act of 1946. The need for such a program became apparent when it was revealed that youth examined at military recruitment stations were suffering from malnutrition or were undernourished.

The national imperative became to feed nutritional meals to poor children and to improve the learning of this at-risk group. Research has found evidence of cognitive impairment resulting from the iron-deficiency anemia often found in poor children (Hunter, 1998).

Grade Levels   All levels

Procedure   The U.S. Department of Agriculture (USDA) administers the NSLP through its Food and Nutrition Service. This organization issues strict dietary guidelines that schools must follow. Participating schools receive cash subsidies and donated commodities in exchange for offering reduced-price or free lunches to low-income children. Students who elect to participate in the program must meet strict family income guidelines. Lunch prices are on a sliding income scale. At the low end of the scale, lunch is free; in the middle, it's subsidized; at the high end, children pay full price.

Barriers to Implementation   The cost of running the NSLP today is over $5 billion. Compared to a cost of $70 million in 1947, the current cost seems staggering. Ironically, it's not the cost that is a barrier to implementation, but the food and the program itself. The stigma of poverty and charity still clouds the school lunch program. Couple that with unappealing meals, and the outcome is much wasted food. The government has given the program several makeovers to combat this problem. Initially, the lunch program was an outlet for surplus agricultural products that could meet nutritional needs, but these foods failed to interest young children. Thanks to a new USDA program—the School Meals Initiative for Healthy Children—children now receive more palatable meals, reflecting new knowledge or dietary needs that have forced the USDA to update its nutritional guidelines (Price & Kuhn, 1996). The National School Lunch Program has become more flexible to include alternative foods, as well as fast food from several fast-food chains. Although children will be receiving traditional fast-food fare of burgers, pizza, tacos, and so on, many of the chain operators have been forced to modify their fare to meet the nutritional standards of the NSLP.

Concerns   A major concern is that children will throw away some of the food, particularly the nutritious food, and opt for the fun food only. Another important concern is that some foods may cause allergic reactions or carry food-borne illnesses.

> *Another social program that has become a school responsibility. It refutes an old adage that "There is no such thing as a free lunch," and develops an atmosphere of irresponsibility. Yet, it is something that cannot be blamed on nor assumed by the student. (Teacher of the Year, Montana)*

Benefits   The benefits of the program certainly outweigh the risks. Millions of poor children have an opportunity to receive a nutritious meal that reduces their risk of cognitive impairment.

> *Kids can't learn if they're hungry. (Teacher of the Year, New Jersey)*

> *We must feed the body before we can feed the mind. (Teacher of the Year, Idaho)*

> *Gives students decent meals who would not get it otherwise. (Teacher of the Year, Hawaii)*

Status   The program is very successful, currently operating in about 100,000 schools, serving millions of students.

Reflections   Current research has illuminated the important role of nutrition in human brain development and learning. Satisfying the need to eat is a very obvious but important factor in learning and development. Maslow (1970) stressed the importance of eating as a basic physiological need that must be satisfied before any higher-order needs are considered. His "hierarchy of needs theory" suggests that children are not very interested in learning if they are hungry. He believed that people were more inclined to satisfy their basic survival needs (food, water, and so on) first and then worry about satisfying aesthetic and intellectual needs. The NSLP continues to spare many poor children the distraction of hunger and allow them to focus on their studies. Recently, some school districts have relaxed the policy of using a sliding income scale to determine who receives a free lunch and who pays for their lunch. Instead, they have opted to give every child a free lunch. I think this policy will do much to alleviate the stigma accompanying a free lunch. Perhaps more children will be willing to accept a free lunch now that they will no longer perceive themselves as being singled out to receive charity.

Paideia Schools

The concept of Paideia schools began with Mortimer Adler's 1930s Paideia Proposal for urban school reform. In the 1980s the Chattanooga School for the Arts and Sciences adopted Mortimer's philosophy to produce the Paideia concept as we know it today. This concept embraces Mortimer's notion of didactic teaching, Socratic questioning, and small-group coaching as an effective model for alternative schooling. In Greek, the term paideia means "the upbringing of a child" (Potter, 1997). The concern for the upbringing of children is reflected in the goals of the Paideia program, which are rooted in Adler's philosophy that education should prepare children to be responsible citizens, to be able to earn a living, and to aspire to be lifelong learners. Underlying learning objectives include but are not limited to recognizing the need for rigor and structure; promoting active, meaningful learning; making the commitment to raising test scores; and encouraging self-competition.

The goals of Paideia schools are to ensure a high-quality education for all children, to increase the number of children that will enter college, and to adequately prepare students to meet the needs of an advanced society. Paideia instructional strategy defers to a discussion of materials (seminaring) and the use of Socratic questioning, a didactic approach to teaching (lecture, textbooks, and films) and coaching that employs a variety of teaching methods.

Seminaring employs three different types of seminars designed to help students work more effectively with teachers: the school seminar, where the faculty and students discuss a specific topic; team seminars, where students and certain teachers meet to discuss disciplinary units as needed; and the classroom seminar, where teachers check for understanding, stimulate interest, and solicit student input.

Materials and Procedures   Mortimer Adler's textbooks usually provide the structural foundation for Paideia inservice or staff development. Paideia schools often use block scheduling and have a coordinating teacher whose sole function is staff development in Paideia instruction. Paideia curriculum strongly resembles that in traditional high schools—four years of English, four years of a foreign language, social studies, science, and the usual electives and extracurricular activities. To strengthen student achievement, the fifth period (in a seven-period day) is reserved for a tutorial period during which students can receive help with any subject.

Barriers to Implementation   Teachers must have a high level of commitment to the program and be willing to spend a great deal of time in staff development (Potter, 1997). They usually have an intense inservice prior to school starting and participate in ongoing training with a Paideia trainer or coordinator assigned to each school. Another barrier might be finding teachers who are committed to the Paideia philosophy and concept.

Concerns   Two problems, high faculty turnover and increased student attrition, appeared after implementing the Paideia concept into the Chattanooga schools. According to Potter (1997), the Paideia project declined to rehire 70 percent of the teachers who reapplied to the Chattanooga High School. Students indicated that they were transferring to easier schools, which increased the normal attrition at Chattanooga.

Benefits   The benefits of the program outweigh the concerns. An impressive 98 percent attendance rate, heightened morale, improved test scores, and higher grade point averages provide sufficient evidence of the success of the Paideia model.

Reflections   I am intrigued by the thought that teachers have so much faith in the Paideia concept, and that they actively seek employment in Paideia-based schools, knowing they will have to devote considerable amounts of time to intensive inservice training. Apparently, they share the fundamental premise of Paideia philosophy as revisited by Adler (1984), which claims that all students can learn all subjects at high levels under the right conditions. It's the use of the word "all" and the absoluteness it suggests that appears problematic. Given cognitive differences—such as learning styles, information processing methods, perceptions, attention spans, and so on—surely caution is recommended when referring to all students and all subjects.

The Paideia concept assumes that success in one setting can be generalized to a somewhat different setting. Of course that's not impossible, but it may be somewhat idealistic. I think it is important to recognize the limitations of any program when evaluating it to determine its success or effectiveness.

Reading Recovery

Reading Recovery is a reading tutorial program initially developed in New Zealand to address low reading achievement. It is a teacher-assisted intervention that targets low-achieving, at-risk readers. Dr. Marie Clay developed the program in the 1970s. It was introduced to the United States in 1974 in what is now known as the National Reading Recovery Center at The Ohio State University. The primary goal of the Reading Recovery program is to bring low-performing readers to grade-level or above using a strategy that integrates a focus on phonological awareness, context clues, and extensive teacher education to facilitate reading. The key to program success is specially trained teachers who can provide effective individualized instruction to at-risk readers.

Grade Levels   The program usually serves the lowest 10–20 percent of low-achieving first graders who are at risk of reading failure.

Materials and Procedures   There are three main components of a Reading Recovery program: training, diagnosing, and tutoring. For the training component, teachers are trained in Reading Recovery procedures in an intensive, year-long training course. They are trained in the theories and practices of effective reading instruction. Most importantly, they are trained to focus on students' strengths, not their deficits.

For the diagnosing component, an examiner administers a survey to each child and the Reading Recovery teacher uses the results to individualize instruction for that child.

In the third component, the tutoring session, Reading Recovery teachers provide daily 30-minute, one-on-one tutorial sessions for up to 20 weeks. Teachers use a detailed analysis of student behavior and knowledge to determine instructional strategy. They can select student reading materials from approximately 2,000 titles of progressive difficulty. The actual tutoring session is comprised of reading known stories, reading a story that was read one time the previous day, writing a story, working with a cut-up sentence, and reading a small new book.

Barriers to Implementation   The program can be very costly in terms of teacher time and training (Hiebert, 1994). A 1996 California audit estimated the cost of teacher leaders at about $18,000 for training, plus conference, travel, and salary compensation (Grossen, Coulter, & Ruggles, 2001, p. 19).

Benefits   In the tutoring sessions, students learn strategies that enable them to become more independent readers. They also learn how to predict, confirm, and understand what they read. The teacher uses "running records" as a form of performance assessment. In this type of assessment, the teacher systematically records the child's activities and uses these observations to inform the instructional basis of subsequent lessons.

> *We have seen great success in the reading level and ability of our younger students. Early intervention is always the key to continued success. (Teacher of the Year, Missouri)*

> *Excellent student participation time. (Teacher of the Year, Idaho)*

Concerns   A major concern is how to effectively transition Reading Recovery students who are successfully discontinued from the program into traditional classroom instruction and have them remain successful. The findings of Pinnell, Lyons, Deford, Bryk, and Seltzer (1994), who reported on the low-achieving child's indispensable need for one-on-one instruction, imply some need for concern.

Research findings indicate that the Reading Recovery program is successful in bringing 75 percent of the student participants at or beyond the reading level of their peers (Sensenbaugh, 1994, p. 2). According to the statistic compiled by the Reading Recovery National Data Evaluation Center, approximately 500,000 children have benefited from Reading Recovery. At least 81 percent of those who had a minimum of 60 lessons were able to successfully become competent, independent readers (School of Teaching and Learning, The Ohio State University, 2000, p. 2). Grossen et al. (2000) charge that the Reading Recovery data reporting is flawed, and that fewer students than are often claimed truly benefit from Reading Recovery. The authors contend that contrary to popular belief, Reading Recovery fails to reduce the need for other compensatory reading services. They cite the inequity in the successful completion of Reading Recovery as evidence of low expectations for children of low socioeconomic status. They also claim that the reported success rate is biased, because children with low expectations of success are removed from the program and are not counted in the calculation of the success rate.

> Reading Recovery is labor intensive, reaching only one child every thirty minutes. We have followed the Ohio/New Zealand model faithfully. Today we have just a few who teach this, as funding is not available. (Teacher of the Year, Idaho)

> Reading Recovery appears to be the better program with farther reaching results, compared to Success For All. Most likely any program that places a teacher in a one-on-one situation with a child is going to work. We like the philosophy of reading behind Reading Recovery better. (Teacher of the Year, Virginia)

Reflections   Reading Recovery appears to be an important program that is certainly addressing a pressing national need—potential reading failure. Reading Recovery is well grounded in research, and the format is appropriate for at-risk children. I think program credibility is endangered by claims that it is excluding "eligible children who are never served and served children who are removed because they do not make adequate progress" (Grossen et al., 2001, p. 3) to inflate its success rate. Such actions, if the allegations are true, defeat the true purpose of the program and only serve to promote the image of Reading Recovery. I would hope that such claims are false, and that Reading Recovery is living up to the fine reputation it has established over the years.

Success For All (SFA)

Success For All (SFA) is a comprehensive, schoolwide reform program serving educationally disadvantaged students. This program offers early intervention for students with learning problems. The goal of the program is to ensure that all children in a high-poverty school will successfully finish the third grade with third-grade reading skills. Success For All was the product of a partnership between the Center for Research on Elementary and Middle Schools and the Baltimore City Public Schools. The program was developed by Robert Slavin (1996), Nancy Madden, and others from Johns Hopkins University. The program went into effect during the 1987–1988 school year in Baltimore schools. The guiding principles of this program are that all children can learn, that early school success is critical for future success, and that learning deficits may be prevented with early intervention. Other goals of the program include reducing the number of students referred to special education, reducing the number of special education referrals, increasing attendance, and providing family support. Success For All has a Spanish, bilingual version for children who are learning English as a second language. They learn to read in Spanish and make the transition to learning in English.

Grade Levels   All students in grades pre-K through 6

Materials and Procedures   Preschoolers attend a half-day program that is designed to enhance the development of their language and school readiness skills. The beginning reading curriculum offers a balanced integration of phonics and comprehension. The full-day kindergarten program emphasizes language, oral and written composition, children's literature, alphabet games, and retelling stories. Cooperative learning is used extensively in the Success For All program.

A period of 90 minutes each day is devoted to reading. In grades K through 1, the emphasis is on language skills development, auditory discrimination, sound blending, and paired reading. Trained, certified teachers work one-on-one tutoring all students in grades 1 through 3 who are having difficulty learning to read. Special emphasis is placed on first-grade students to prevent the need for remediation.

In special education, every effort is made to address and eliminate a student's learning problems, using tutoring within the regular classroom. Tutors evaluate students' needs and develop instructional strategies tailored to meet those individual needs.

Students are assessed every 8 weeks to ascertain their reading progress. Family support teams comprised of the principal, a facilitator, a social worker, and other appropriate personnel work with families to ensure each child succeeds. Some family support teams provide community or mental health services at the school, or they refer the families to appropriate agencies. A full-time facilitator works in each SFA school to help teachers implement the reading program, to coordinate the 8-week assessments, to plan and implement staff development, and to assist the family support team. Teachers and trainers receive three days of inservice training at the beginning of each school year. They receive extensive training throughout the school year. The principal, the facilitator, teachers, the social worker, and research staff meet weekly as an advisory committee to review program progress.

Barriers to Implementation   The SFA program is thought to be costly, depending on the level of implementation. However, program costs may be offset by the reduction in special education referrals and placements. The use of certified teachers as tutors also reduces costs.

Concerns   Some critics of SFA contend that the program is not meeting its intended goal of ensuring that all children will be performing at grade level in reading by the time they complete third grade. In 1991, nearly 40 percent of third graders in the program remained from 1 month to 1 year below grade level (Office of Education Research [OER], 1993, p. 3). Despite this criticism, assessment results indicate that it is a very successful program. It seems reasonable to conclude that SFA programs are moving closer to meeting their goals.

> *Success For All is a pricey program. Only studies done are by the company, or those linked to it. Who wouldn't do well with one-to-one tutoring? (Teacher of the Year, Virginia)*

Benefits   Few alternative reading programs have been as successful as SFA in increasing reading performance. As an added benefit, SFA has been effective in reducing special education placements.

Reflections   Success For All, or helping all children experience success, is such a worthwhile, important goal. Yet the question looms large whether this is an achievable goal, particularly when there is a time constraint. Some children may take longer than third grade to "catch up" and experience success, particularly those children who are experiencing a developmental lag. The use of time constraints ignores the acknowledged benefits of providing individualized instruction and of accommodating learning styles. Another concern with time constraints is whether there could be such a focus on meeting the end goal that teachers, in trying to save time, omit important repetitions in instruction and variations in instructional strategy. Unfortunately, time constraints are an essential, important factor in program evaluation, and they are not likely to go away.

Trailblazers

Trailblazers is a decentralized camping program that serves disadvantaged, underprivileged youth in urban settings of New York and New Jersey. John A. Mitchell founded the program in 1887 after raising $800. Through a joint philanthropic effort of the Duke Foundation, Doris Duke, and the New Jersey Nature Conservancy, the program was moved to a site featuring 1,000 forested acres, complete with a 55-acre lake.

The program uses an experiential education model that seeks to educate the whole child. Children live in teepees, hogans, or covered wagons in small communities headed by a volunteer group leader. The group leaders, who are recruited from all over the world, serve in 10-week terms. The organization makes a 3-year commitment to each child who participates in the program. Program goals are to empower and foster the development of each child emotionally, intellectually, physically, and socially. Social workers, teachers, or counselors usually refer children. Trailblazers provides a unique opportunity for children to develop empathy and cooperation; to practice healthy, wholesome living; to gain respect for the environment; and to enjoy learning and living close to nature. This distinguished, award-winning program has thrived over its 115-year tenure. The future of this program looks bright as it continues to serve disadvantaged children (Trailblazers, 2000).

3

Policies

*School policy is a plan of action to determine which pro-
cedures should be followed in a given situation and what
actions should be taken if the policy is violated.*

**"Our zero-tolerance policy is unfair. In the
school play, I play a student who gets an F in math.
The principal suspended me from the team until
my character brings his grades up."**

Honor Roll

Honor roll is usually a public display of names of people whose accomplishments in one or more areas warrant recognition. The school honor roll is a tradition that recognizes qualities and behaviors that are valued by traditional educators. Students are usually recognized for their achievement or attendance. Sometimes they are recognized for their attitude; and on rare occasions, they are recognized for their behavior. The concept of honoring students has been extended to honoring teachers, parents, and schools. Honor rolls are used not just to incentivise and to motivate students to achieve and make good grades but also to encourage parents to become more involved in their children's studies.

Although honor rolls generally enjoy a good reputation, they do have some limitations that are a cause for concern. The issue of fairness is a concern because honor-roll policy and standards are set at the level of each individual school; there are no districtwide or countywide standards for honor-roll status. Malawer (1994) characterizes honor rolls as being unfair and superfluous. He accuses them of being exclusionary in that they fail to consider student diversity. He criticizes the policy of rewarding only the students who embrace school values and interests. He charges that honor rolls dishonor some students, particularly those with disabilities. Special education students are automatically excluded from participation in most honor-roll programs. Their classes are weighted less than traditional classes, which will always result in the special education student missing the required 3.0 GPA for honor-roll status (Schnaiberg, 1997).

Many people view honor rolls as elitist, which breeds resentment in students and parents. The popularity of the bumper sticker, "My D student beat up your honor-roll student" reflects the resentment and hostility aimed at the honor-roll policy. Although the student may have used intrinsic motivation to achieve the honor roll, honor rolls are thought to be extrinsic motivators. A final criticism is that honor rolls stress competition with others, rather than competition with oneself. That is not all bad, because it mirrors the competitive structure of the real world.

Overall, honor rolls are very effective for those who are able and willing to do the work.

Immersion

Immersion education is usually associated with learning a foreign language. As the term *immersion* suggests, the learner is placed in a setting where initially, the only language spoken is the foreign language. The foreign language is spoken 100 percent of the time to maximize the student's exposure to the new language.

Supporters of the immersion policy believe that students will learn more language, more efficiently. They will avoid just learning words and grammar, and translating. Pausing to translate is believed to slow down the learning of language. It is believed that by being immersed in the language, students will be able to carry on conversations more effectively. Many consider the immersion approach superior to the audio-lingual approach used in the 1960s, in which students memorized and recited dialogue from audiotapes. Approximately 300,000 students are participating in various types of immersion programs, which are distinguished by when and how students learn a new language (Reyhner, 1998, p. 1).

Partial immersion programs will have students alternate between their native language and the language to be learned, using the second language at least 50 percent of the time.

Early immersion students begin learning language as early as preschool; late immersion students may begin as late as high school. Two-way immersion programs have 50 percent of the class speaking one native language and 50 percent of the class speaking another native language. Teachers alternate between the two languages when teaching. Students support each other in their attempts to learn the new language.

Immersion has its drawbacks. Full immersion, in which speaking the native language is not allowed, may have the consequence of traumatizing children. Parents often contribute to that trauma by punishing the student if they speak in their native language. They want to assure their children of a place in mainstream America. Another disadvantage of immersion is that students who demonstrate a lack of fluency in the dominant language may be viewed as deficient.

Partial immersion seems to be the preferred method of introducing students to a new language. It preserves the dignity of the native language as it stresses the importance of the new language.

Inclusion

Inclusion is a fairly recent educational innovation, fostered by reforms in public policy. Inclusion conceptually embraces a philosophy of providing the maximum education possible for students with a handicapping condition, in the least restrictive environment. A clear definition of inclusion has yet to be established. Phi Delta Kappa's Center for Evaluation, in its 1993 Research Bulletin 11 (Stout, 1996), has made an effort to disentangle the definitions of mainstreaming, inclusion, and full inclusion to clarify the concepts. Mainstreaming involves selective placement of students that is determined by a student's potential and ability to function in a regular classroom. Inclusion involves putting the child in the regular classroom and bringing the support services to the child. Full inclusion, which is probably the most contentious, mandates that all students, regardless of the severity of their condition, will be in a regular classroom full-time. No cost is spared to bring needed services to the classroom for those students.

The origins of inclusion date back to the 1960s (Conderman, 1998). The practice gained momentum in 1975 with the Education for All Handicapped Children Act (EAHCA), which granted all children the right to a public education. In the 1980s, the Regular Education Initiative called for a unified system of education that would necessarily entail a merger of special and regular education. In the 1990s, the government changed and renamed the EAHCA to IDEA, or the Individuals with Disabilities Education Act. That reform includes six premises (Petch-Hogan & Haggard, 1999):

1. Disabled children have a right to an education.
2. An appropriate education will be determined by a child's strengths and weaknesses.
3. All children will be encouraged to develop to their full potential.
4. Each child has a right to associate with nondisabled peers.
5. All children will be made aware of their differences and strengths to promote full integration into society.
6. Reducing the stigma of labeling and placement should enhance the social status of the disabled.

The advent of full inclusion precipitated heavy debates in the educational forum. Parents, teacher administrators, and legislators were either advocates or opponents of inclusion.

Proponents argue that inclusion will meet individual students' needs using trained teachers and individualized education plans. They stress the importance of opportunity for exposure to same-age peers. Opponents assert that inclusion may not meet individual student needs because teachers may not have adequate training, some teachers may not have a positive attitude toward inclusion, and special needs children may not be readily accepted socially. Critics are skeptical of the effectiveness of inclusion, considering an obvious lack of empirical evidence to support it. Some educators adamantly object to inclusion, arguing that it forces them to sacrifice the needs of the many for the needs of the few. However, most educators agree that inclusion does contribute to the overarching goals of education—to educate all children.

Individualized Education Plan

IEP is an acronym for the Individualized Education Plan (IEP) for exceptional students. This is a documented plan that details the special education, present achievement levels, goals, related services, and strategies for these students. This plan is mandated by law and is a necessary component of school policy. Parents, teachers, specialists, and in some cases the student and a child advocate work together to develop the plan. The IEP is updated annually to ascertain the student's current level of functioning, goals for the year, need for special services, level of participation, and a detailed schedule of objectives and assessment. The IEP is confidential, and parents have the right to challenge it if they think it unsuitable for their child.

Intelligence Testing

IQ testing, or intelligence testing, was introduced in the United States in 1912 with the advent of the *Stanford-Binet Intelligence Test.* A child's IQ (intelligence quotient) was determined by a ratio of a calculated mental age and the child's chronological age, multiplied by 100. Mental age is determined by the child's stopping point on a series of age-appropriate tasks on the test. If, for example, a child had a mental age score of 12 and a chronological age score of 10, that child's IQ would be 120 (IQ = 12/10 ¥ 100 = 120). The average IQ is 100. The IQ in this example is considered above average. Numerous group and individual intelligence tests have appeared on the assessment scene since the introduction of the *Stanford-Binet.*

Currently, IQ testing—particularly group testing—has lost favor in many school districts. One California school district has banned group testing since 1960 (Law, 1995). Many school districts have changed their policy of widespread testing in the wake of the firestorm of charges of cultural and ethnic bias in testing. Hot debates continue to fuel controversies over misinterpretation of test scores, inappropriate uses of tests, examiner bias, inaccuracy of results, the potential for discrimination, and unpopular theories of ethnic inferiority.

Despite the furor, intelligence tests are still used to identify gifted students and special education students. Caution and fairness are the watchwords of testing. Test makers strive to create more culture-free tests, although it is questionable whether that is possible. Educators are warned not to rely on one test score to make decisions about a child's academic fate. Instead, they are encouraged to use a battery of tests. New theories such as self-efficacy and multiple intelligences are being used to assess student intelligence in some districts. The trend is toward more individualized testing and the use of a new deviation IQ that counters the problem of inaccurate interpretation of scores as children age. A child's deviation IQ is determined by comparing their performance to that of other students in their age group.

No Pass/No Play

The Texas House Bill No. 72 of 1985 paved the way for the notorious No Pass/No Play legislation that limits students' participation in extracurricular activities if they fail to meet the academic standards set forth by their school districts, or if they fail one or more courses. The roots of this legislation go back to the beginning of the 20th century, when athletics became more visible and appreciated than academics. During that time, the concept of extracurricular (or outside the regular curriculum) was conceived: Athletics fell outside the core subjects of math, history, reading, and so on. This divergence of curriculums would generate controversy for the next several decades as the opponents of athletics touted the negative effects of extracurricular activities on academics.

The effects of this legislation have been far-reaching, affecting both intended and unintended groups. Currently, it affects students with disabilities, students in advanced placement classes—almost any student who represents the school in almost any extracurricular activity, including drama and chess competitions, drill teams, and so on (Davis, 1996).

The primary objective or intent of those supporting the no pass, no play policy was to motivate students to pay attention to academics, to maintain or improve their grades, and to establish appropriate priorities. Initial penalties associated with this policy were severe. In some cases, if a student was failing one course, that student would be barred from participating in the activity for 6 weeks. The definition of *participation* was broad; it meant they could not compete, they could not practice, and they could not assist with performances or have a role in a one-act play, travel with the teams, take photos, or be recognized with their teams or organizations (Davis, 1996).

The effect of the new policy was so severe that opponents challenged it in court—to no avail. The courts ruled in favor of the states' right to use whatever means necessary to increase the academic performance of its student constituency (Cooke, 1992). The courts did not view the policy as a violation of student's rights. In the late nineties, the legislature did enact a revision of the law. No Pass/No Play legislation was still the core of the policy, but the ineligibility period was reduced from 6 weeks to 3 weeks. According to Burnett (2001), the policy has spawned a host of indirect effects, including cheating, opting for less challenging classes, watering down courses, and so on. The most devastating effects of this policy are its contribution to the dropout rate. Burnett (2001) contends that athletics may be the sole reason that some students have any interest in school. When their reason leaves, they often leave with it. Sweet (1986) points out that the No Pass/No Play policy has had an overwhelmingly disproportionate effect on poor, young, black males—more so than on any other group. Although the policy may benefit some students, opponents propose that we have yet to see the end of the inequities and indirect effects, abuses of the system, further alienation of students, and continued divisiveness of athletics versus academics. Perhaps further revision and consideration of the No Pass/No Play rule will give this policy the ability to serve as the positive motivator it was originally intended to be and sufficiently minimize any negative long-term effects in the process.

Resource Room

The 1975 Education for All Handicapped Children Act (EHACA) mandated that all children, regardless of challenges or disabilities, be guaranteed a free, appropriate education. Because of this mandate, several million children with special needs would require special services (Council for Exceptional Children, 1989). By law, each one of the millions of children served would require an IEP (Individualized Education Plan). The resource room, a special classroom designed to provide for special needs students, is usually a very important part of these students' IEPs.

Resource classrooms are usually staffed with specially trained resource teachers, who assist students as determined by their IEP. The resource teacher's role is to offer special materials and assistance to the regular classroom teachers who teach special needs children. Resource teachers usually have a competency in a particular area, such as special education or remedial reading. The types of teaching activities determine the classification of the resource room as tutorial, prevocational, content area, basic skills, coping skills, or consultation (Reith & Ocala, 1984).

Students with disabilities are served in one of six possible educational environments: regular class, resource room, separate class, separate school, residential facility, or homebound/hospital placements. Resource rooms provide service for students who may spend part of their school day in a regular classroom and usually spend at least 21 percent but not more than 60 percent of their day in the resource room (Office of Special Education Programs, 1995, p. 1).

Sexual Harassment

Several decades ago, it was not unusual when a male student touched a female student on the private parts of her body. There seemed to be a high tolerance for this type of behavior; the saying "boys will be boys" was an accepted adage that reflected the sentiment of the times. The turn of the century brought with it a shift in sentiment, kindling a new movement in the treatment of behavior that can be classified as sexually harassing. The Supreme Court decided that students sexually harassing other students would no longer be tolerated.

This movement, like many other movements, was sparked by a significant incident. The lawsuit of *Aurelia Davis v. Monroe County Board of Education* (May 1999) was filed on behalf of a fifth-grade girl whose family alleged that a male student had been sexually harassing her for a long time. The Supreme Court ruled that schools or their representatives who failed to respond to charges of serious sexual harassment could be sued under Title IX (Gorney, 1999). The Supreme Court ruling held that sexual harassment could interfere with student learning. Students would be entitled to collect monetary damages from schools or school officials if the school had known of the harassment and ignored it. Title IX of the Education Amendments of 1972 guarantees students protection from sexual harassment in schools (Crumpler, 1993).

It is not surprising that attempts to solve a problem frequently generate new problems. A big problem in sexual harassment cases is in determining exactly what constitutes sexual harassment. The Equal Employment Opportunity Commission recognizes two types of sexual harassment that can conceptually be used in claims of harassment. One type, "quid pro quo" (something for something), occurs, for example, when a superior seeks sex for a favorable promotion decision. Another type of sexual harassment is "hostile environment," where unwelcome sexual advances create an offensive environment (Huston, 1993). I think the latter type is more likely to be found in schools. What may once have been viewed as a harmless prank will be clouded by the dark overtone of this new legislation and aggressively dealt with.

Schools will no longer turn a blind eye or a deaf ear to claims. They will not want to invite lawsuits. They will act swiftly and assertively. Unfortunately, several ambiguities confound the question of whether a behavior or comment is—or is not—sexually harassing. Some people in a position to judge want to consider voice inflection, tone of voice, gestures, and other fine lines of discernment. To protect themselves from litigation, educational institutions are willing to paint sexual harassment with a very broad brush to include anything and everything that may be considered sexually harassing. Sexual advances such as unwanted grabbing, touching, hugging, fondling, lewd comments, suggestive remarks, intimate or sexual jokes, showing pornography or sexual cartoons, commenting on a person's body, spreading sexual rumors, or making sexual gestures or signs will all serve to broaden the brush stroke.

Fine lines and broad criteria offer much opportunity for abuse and/or discrimination, particularly when it is difficult to determine a person's intent or motive. Having to infer intent, when judgment may be clouded by fear of legal action, often invites disaster. Under these circumstances, typically harmless gestures and behaviors may easily be misinterpreted or misconstrued.

The final dilemma is: What should be done? Which behaviors merit a warning and which merit harsh action? Should consequences be age-appropriate, or should a 5-year-old boy be expelled from school for kissing a little girl and receive the same treatment as an adult male who kisses a woman? Such questions beg for answers, but defy easy solution. Will fear of sexual harassment charges be the end of the courting and the puppy love that often begins in seventh or eighth grades? Perhaps part of the answer is to teach young children appropriate ways to court, flirt, or seek the attention of the opposite sex. Hopefully, once the fear of lawsuits quiets, maybe we can achieve some balance in this issue of sexual harassment and some assurance that the punishment will fit the crime—if indeed a crime has been committed.

Standardized Testing

Popham (1999) defines a standardized test as an examination that uses the same predetermined administration and scoring procedures for each test. Standardized testing is usually conducted nationwide, using large sample groups to develop norms. It is assumed that the development of test items and the interpretation of test scores are conducted in a predetermined, uniform manner. There are a large variety of standardized tests, which fall into three broad categories of achievement aptitude, and diagnostics. The SAT and the ACT are well-known, widely used aptitude tests designed to predict how a student will do in various educational settings. IQ tests such as the *Stanford-Binet* and the *Wechsler* scales are also important aptitude tests. Achievement tests such as the *California Achievement Tests*, the *Comprehensive Tests of Basic Skills*, and the *Iowa Test of Basic Skills* are designed to measure what and how much a student has learned. Diagnostic tests such as the *Frosting Developmental Test of Visual Perception* are designed to ascertain a student's level of competence in a particular content area.

The collective purposes of standardized tests are to diagnose weaknesses or strengths, to assess what a student has learned, or to predict future success (or a lack of it) in an educational setting in such a way that a person can make a reliable and valid inference about the results.

Numerous criticisms and issues surrounding standardized testing have made it one of the hottest educational issues of the past few decades. The notion of "high-stakes" testing Kohn (2000) has added a new dimension of fear to the standardized testing movement. Teachers are afraid of losing their jobs, students fear they won't graduate, and schools are afraid that they will be closed and disbanded. All three share the same source of fear—low standardized test scores. A major criticism of standardized testing is an overemphasis on test scores to evaluate the quality of teaching and learning. This national focus on test scores is fueled by demands for teacher accountability and tough standards and driven by the corporate pursuit of profit. Most standardized testing operations are owned by corporations eager to capitalize on the increased demands for more and tougher testing. A television documentary revealed that some test producers had difficulties filling orders on time. They were overwhelmed by the sheer volume of requests. The cost of testing is another source of criticism.

Opponents of standardized testing question whether test developers can adequately and fairly assess intelligence, achievement, and aptitude. Asa Hilliard (2000) questions the predictive validity of standardized tests when examined in the light of student success where failure was initially predicted. The validity of achievement tests is also questioned, because there is no national curriculum to establish the validity of a nationally standardized test.

Another strong criticism is test bias, which has long been thought to be a viable explanation for the "test score gap" that exists between whites and African Americans, and between whites and Mexican Americans. Test bias has many faces—cultural, language, and socioeconomic. African American and Hispanic students feel the barbs of test bias most often. The inequity of test preparation, as when the more affluent students can pay test-prep companies for a guaranteed improved score, is a socioeconomic bias. Test developers prepare test items whose content extends beyond the classroom into the realm of the dominant culture, increasing the probability of higher test scores for students of the dominant culture. Language also is a barrier and source of bias, particularly for Latino or Mexican American students.

Alfie Kohn (2000a) contends that standardized tests hurt students of color more so than other groups. Students of color, many of them at risk for failure, are the ones who need help the most. Kohn also thinks high-stakes testing is a form of educational ethnic cleansing (2000b). There is a sort of domino effect that adversely affects children of color. Teachers are pressured to raise scores, and students become the recipients of a diminished curriculum as more teachers align their teaching with the test and possibly ignore other subjects. In such cases, where standards are lowered to raise test scores, children of color may receive a watered-down curriculum that pushes them further down the achievement scale and effectively widens the test score gap between them and their white counterparts. If these children are younger than 8 or 9 years old, their already numerous academic risks are increased. Like many other researchers, Perrone (1991) is against testing young children in their formative years, when they should be exposed to a variety of content and encouraged to engage in higher levels of thinking.

Standardized tests are criticized for their extensive use of multiple-choice and true-false questions. These question types are criticized because their content usually falls into the lowest level of Benjamin Bloom's (1956) taxonomy of instructional objectives, emphasizing memorization and recall. Despite the criticisms, standardized testing has its share of proponents. That number is growing exponentially now that testing is such a political issue. Proponents cite improved test scores in states like Texas, the home of the infamous *Texas Assessment of Academic Skills* (TAAS) test. Failure to pass this test has kept many students from graduating. It is this sort of scenario, the use of a single test score to make such an important decision as graduation, that pushes me into the ranks of those who question standardized testing. I think testing should be put into perspective and interpreted only as a small indicator of a student's ability, achievement, and so on, at a given time, within a particular context. To be fair and accurate, testing should be aligned with teaching objectives. An assessment battery is preferable to using a single score to determine student's needs and to assure fair placement. Authentic and alternative assessment can be effective complements or substitutes for standardized tests, but which will be used is usually at the teacher's discretion.

Summer School

Many schools have adopted a policy of holding school in the summer during summer vacation. Extending the instructional program beyond the school year is designed to help underachievers raise their scores and improve their performance. Summer school is more desirable than retention. Some schools districts have a mandatory summer school attendance policy for low achievers. Others resist the mandatory attendance approach, believing that students may be unruly or resistant if they are forced to attend summer school. Many school districts prefer a moderate approach; they strongly recommend summer school and offer incentives, extend invitations, or develop compelling programs to attract students. Convincing students to attend summer school is difficult, particularly considering that students have so many pleasurable options during the summer.

Cost is a factor in determining which, and how many, students may attend. Low achievers usually have priority. An important positive benefit of summer school is that it may help students avoid failing and the consequential social stigma of being retained. Summer school can be an enrichment activity for all students, providing productive engagement in lieu of the boredom and idleness that often accompany summer vacation. Studies have shown that summer school can be effective in improving scores, bringing students up to grade level, and honing basic skills (Chmelynski, 1998).

Teacher Accountability

Nationwide, the erosion of confidence in teacher competence has issued a call for teacher accountability. Many believe that teachers should be accountable for their performance in the classroom, much like business-people are held accountable for their work. A great source of controversy is how to determine a teacher's effectiveness in the classroom. Many people believe that the best way to measure accountability is to determine teacher success in terms of student success or student test scores. Others recognize that several variables may affect test scores, and that teachers should be evaluated only on factors under their control, not for students' poor performance on test scores. Some people believe that teachers are already accountable, and that students must share some of the responsibility for their own education. Most people believe that teachers who are not performing well should receive training, mentoring, and incentives, if necessary. However, others believe that low-performing teachers should not be retained.

The controversy surrounding teacher accountability has raged for the past few decades, ebbing and flowing in political importance and instigating a plethora of related legislation. According to the California Teachers Association (1998, p. 1), at least 34 urban school districts in at least 32 states have teacher accountability systems. A push for a national system of teacher accountability is gaining momentum, thanks to current politics. Politicians are responding to the public demand for accountability with partisan plans to establish a teacher accountability system based on student test results as well as teacher test results.

Another question looming over the issue of teacher accountability is what constitutes a fair assessment of teacher effectiveness. Hawley (Board on Teacher Assessment of National Academy of Sciences, 1999) suggests that there are five major approaches to teacher assessment: (1) basic skills, (2) general knowledge tests, (3) content knowledge test, (4) tests of pedagogical knowledge, and (5) performance assessment (p. 1). The ambiguous educational descriptions of tasks and the multitasking involved in teaching make it difficult to develop a fair instrument. Critics of teacher accountability contend that to be fair, teacher testing should be in alignment with educational standards, curriculum objectives, and frameworks.

The California Teaching Association (1999) offers some good policy considerations that could refine the fairness issues: The purpose of accountability should be to improve the quality of education; (2) accountability should be aligned with district standards, objectives, and so on; (3) staff development should be an important part of accountability; (4) accountability is a shared responsibility among teachers, students, parents, administrators, and the community; and (5) teachers should be accountable only to the extent of their ability to make educational decisions and to control relevant factors affecting their performance.

A host of problems have evolved from the issue of accountability. Should merit pay be granted or denied? Should teachers receive assistance or be removed from their job? Should low-performing schools become wards of the state? How far should we go with high-stakes testing? The quest is on to find appropriate answers to these questions. Over the next few years, we can expect that more states will develop some sort of accountability program. This current educational policy is an important trend that is not going away any time soon.

Zero Tolerance

The policy of "zero tolerance" began in 1994 with the advent of P.L. 103–382 or the Gun-Free Schools Act (Pipho, 1998) passed by the federal government. This law was enacted to require mandatory expulsion for anyone bringing a gun to school. The purpose of this law was to send a strong message to those who would consider bringing a weapon to school that such an act would not be tolerated under any circumstances. States and school districts expanded the concept beyond guns to include any potentially dangerous weapons, liquor, controlled substances, robbery, assault, and extortion. The aim of zero tolerance is safe schools for all children.

The penalty for violation of the law is a 1-year expulsion from school that in some cases may be modified by a school district's administration. States were coerced into compliance by making access to ESEA (Elementary and Secondary Education Act) funds contingent on compliance with P.L. 103–382. Although many school districts have reported some success with zero tolerance, there are some inherent problems in the policy. One is in clearly defining the term *weapon*—is it limited to guns, or is it broader? Without clear definition, it is difficult to apply the law fairly. For example, would a small paring knife carry the same penalty as a gun? A grenade is not a gun; should it be exempt? Another problem is that of mandatory expulsion versus mandatory attendance. These policies are contradictory, because they both have funding contingencies that place the school at odds with itself. If students are expelled under mandatory expulsion, they cannot be counted in the mandatory attendance requirement. It becomes a no-win situation; if a student violates the law, the school district loses money under mandatory attendance if it complies with mandatory expulsion, and it loses money from ESEA if it does not comply.

A third problem is the possibility of having a penalty that is much more serious than an offense warrants, such as in the case of a student bringing prescription medication to school. Expulsion for a year would be excessive.

Opponents of zero tolerance oppose the notion of treating all situations the same regardless of circumstances. Curwin and Mendler (1998) advocated fairness over tough policy. Efforts are under way to encourage legislative bodies to broaden definitions and develop guidelines and procedures that will maintain the integrity of zero tolerance, but that would give more discretion to school administrators, encouraging them to use judgment and consider circumstances.

4

Philosophies, Theories, and Movements

Educational movements are trends or tendencies to try new and different ideas and theories.

"In an increasingly complex world, sometimes old questions require new answers."

Alternative Assessment

The movement toward alternative assessment began as early as 1934, according to Ralph W. Tyler (interview in Horowitz, 1995). Tyler felt that there was too much dependence on one single assessment at that time. Historically, assessment was either paper-and-pencil or machine-scored tests. Alternative assessment is a response to the demand for alternatives to written multiple-choice tests. Like Tyler, other educators began to question the value, validity, and accuracy of traditional assessment. They wanted assessment that emphasized the development of students, was authentic and reflected real life, and accurately depicted a child's progress toward educational goals and successful performance.

Educators also wanted assessment that would be useful for guiding instruction and gauging teacher effectiveness. Alternative assessment was a response to this need for accountability. The call for assessment reform or the revision of evaluation practices began with the publication titled *Curriculum and Evaluation for School Mathematics* (National Council of Teachers of Mathematics [NCTM], 1989), which advocated changes in thinking about the assessment of math. Educators needed a more inclusive, holistic measure of student knowledge—a measure that paper-and-pencil tests could not adequately provide. Obviously, alternative assessment can be defined as any assessment other than the traditional pencil-and-paper or scanned assessment. Cronbach (1960) refines the definition by proposing that alternative assessment involves using several techniques to observe students' performance and gather other diverse information. Alternative measures that are currently popular include portfolios, which give teachers and parents a long-term depiction of student performance, and authentic assessment, for a more real-world assessment of student abilities.

Short (1993) proposes incorporating alternative measures into lesson plans to give students an opportunity to demonstrate knowledge. These measures should employ a variety of assessment tools that meet individual needs. Students should be aware of assessment objectives prior to the lesson. Alternative assessment comes in various modes and mediums. Tannenbaum (2000) identified five types of nonverbal assessment strategies:

- Pictorial products—picture graphs and models
- Physical demonstrations—thumbs up and thumbs down for yes and no
- KWL charts—Know, Wants to know, Learned
- Oral and written products
- Oral performance or presentation

Short (1993, p. 6) offers the following alternative assessment measures: "skills checklists, reading and writing inventories, anecdotal rewards, teacher observations, student self-evaluations, portfolios, performance-based tasks, essay writing, oral reports, and interviews." Other popular forms include video recordings, oral retelling, anecdotal notes, running records, and checklists. The goal of alternative assessments is to create an accurate picture of a learner's progress at a particular point in time. This new movement is clouded with concerns and controversy. For example, what source should teachers rely on when test scores and nontraditional assessment conflict (Wolf, LeMahieu, & Eresh, 1992)? Parents are concerned about high schools' willingness to accept non-traditional assessments such as portfolios. Researchers raise questions of validity, reliability, equity, and fairness. I believe alternative assessment will continue to grow in popularity as long as there are no demonstrated negative effects on student achievement and promotion.

Brain-Based Learning

Brain research has become so important to education and our society that in 1990, President George H. Bush declared the years 1990–2000 the "Decade of the Brain" by signing a presidential proclamation (Library of Congress, 2000). The purpose of the proclamation is to inform the public about the results of brain research and to use the research in programs and activities that would benefit the public. Brain-based learning is an effort to use brain research to improve education. It uses current neuroscientific research to develop principles about how the brain works and how that knowledge can be used to better inform teaching. It also explains the effects of brain activity on learning and the role of teachers and the class environment in brain-based learning. The need for brain-based learning is supported by some educators and researchers, who believe that traditional education stifles and discourages the way the brain actually learns.

Research on various aspects of the brain and factors that affect it have important implications for learning and cognition. Some of those factors are (Jensen, 2001):

- The brain's ability to regenerate itself
- The effects of stress and the effect of hormones on brain function
- The benefits of neural plasticity, which can change the way learning occurs, in understanding attention and attention deficit
- The import of threat on the brain
- The effect of music on the brain
- The role of nutrition in brain functioning
- The effect of chemicals on the brain
- The abilities of the very young brain

Caine and Caine (1994) identified 12 core principles of brain-based learning:

1. The brain can perform several activities at once; it is a parallel processor.
2. Learning engages the entire physiology of the learner.
3. The search for meaning is inborn or innate.
4. Patterning facilitates the search for meaning.
5. Emotions have a critical role in patterning.
6. The brain processes parts and wholes simultaneously.
7. Attention and peripheral perception are important parts of learning.
8. Learning involves conscious and unconscious processes.
9. The brain features two types of memory: spatial and rote.
10. Facts imbedded in spatial memory are best remembered and understood.
11. Challenge enhances learning; threat inhibits it.
12. All brains are unique.

All of the principles have been important contributors to informing teacher behavior and implementing change. Many teachers have changed their classroom environments in an effort to make them more brain-friendly. The effect of threat on learning has caused many teachers to rethink the way they discipline, motivate, and interact with their students. Teachers realize that they can control the threat they pose to their student, so they try to minimize it. Poole (1997) identified threats from environmental factors outside of the classroom, such as poverty, family violence, and abuse. He contends that these factors have a powerful negative effect on children's thinking. Resource people in the schools may be able to minimize the threat to children, posed by environmental factors. Some teachers are employing innovative strategies, such as scenting their environment. Gabriel (1999) contends that in the scented environment, students were less likely to need redirecting. Some teachers employed practical, functional strategies such as letting students keep a bottle of water, with the understanding that they would have to go to the restroom more often.

Brain-based learning, like most theories, is not without critics. Some think it is just a fad, that it does not work, and that it has nothing new to offer. Others laud brain-based learning as an important change agent in their lives. Jensen (2001) recommends caution in considering these claims about brain-based learning, warning that they do not "prove" anything; however, research does show strong evidence of positive results.

Conditions of Learning

Robert Gagné (1970) developed a theory of instruction that identifies five categories of learning outcomes, organized by what is being learned: intellectual skills, verbal information, cognitive strategies, attitudes, and motor skills. Gagné looked at conditions that facilitate learning to determine the best approach to be used for teaching. By carefully observing what goes on during instruction, he identified nine events of instruction. His theory was that an analysis of instruction would reveal its parts, which should be stated as performance objectives and taught sequentially. Gagné's nine sequential instructional events are rooted in information processing theory (indicated in parentheses):

1. Gain the attention of the learner (reception).
2. State the objectives in terms of expected performance outcomes (expectancy).
3. Stimulate recall of relevant prior learning (retrieval).
4. Present the stimulus needed for learning (selective perception).
5. Provide learning guidance (semantic encoding).
6. Elicit performance from the learner (responding).
7. Provide feedback on the performance (reinforcement).
8. Assess the performance of the learner (retrieval).
9. Enhance retention and transfer of learning (generalization).

These events of instruction were designed to provide teachers with a guide for instruction. Teachers often use this format and sequence in planning lessons.

Gagné's theory is primarily behaviorist, with a cognitive slant. It is teacher-centered. Now that constructivism has gained popularity, it has stolen the luster of many such behaviorist-oriented programs. Constructivism is learner-centered and advocates that the teacher act as a facilitator to help students construct their own meanings. Currently it is the preferred approach.

Internet

The Internet came into being in 1982 as a result of the ARPANET, an international network of computer networks linked by cables. Each network is capable of operating independently. Within these networks are routers or gateways, which through interconnections link it to the outside world. Gateways are large computers designed to handle a large volume of traffic. The handling of data is analogous to handling packages in a transportation system, in which each data package has an address. Special software is used on these networks to help route packages to their appropriate destination using TCP/IP (transmission control protocol/internet protocol) telecommunications protocol to transfer data. The Internet is so fast and powerful that it can transfer data anywhere in the world in seconds.

To facilitate the many uses of the Internet, a variety of protocols, or common languages that allow different networks to communicate with each other, are used. The Internet and the World Wide Web are not synonymous.

The Net is a tangible network of computers, whereas the Web is an imaginary space of information connected by hypertext links in the form of sounds, graphics, videos, data, and so on. It is impossible for the Web to exist without the Net (Griffiths, 1999). The Web is used for retrieving and disseminating data, text, or multimedia files via the Internet. The user has to have an Internet connection, usually a modem and special browser software installed on their computer, to access information or files on the Net. A huge array of search engines is now available on the Internet to facilitate the information search process.

Internet usage has grown exponentially over the years, as computer users have found more and more uses for it. Here are some ways we currently use the Internet:

- Purchase goods
- Do online banking (includes paying bills and transferring funds)
- Make investments such as purchasing stocks and mutual funds
- Monitor investments, get stock quotes, and research stocks
- Conduct video conferences all over the world
- Review movies, get news, and listen to music
- Socialize in chat rooms
- Take virtual trips to other countries
- Take classes online through distance learning and virtual classrooms
- Get maps for a particular location, or locate people
- Browse for general information
- Do research for papers
- Post information to virtual bulletin boards
- Link to Web sites for educational information and resources such as lesson plans
- Send electronic mail and attach documents
- Sell products

The Internet has changed the world, how we think, and how we live. Some words of caution are needed regarding the many facets of Internet usage—the great, the bad, and the very ugly. The great news is that everyone loves it, young and old. The Net is great for education because it motivates, and it improves research skills. It increases access to vast resources at minimal cost. El Hindi (1998) points out that Internet usage is making educators rethink and redefine literacy and learning. The bad news is that the costs of software, hardware, rewiring, and renovation may be beyond the limited budgets of many schools. Some schools cannot afford the additional expense of the virus protection and needed software upgrades. Affluent schools are more likely to be connected to the Internet than poorer schools. Teacher training is a budget issue and a time concern. Despite these problems, teacher training is imperative; students as young as first grade are quite facile with the computer, and older students are often more facile than teachers. This is especially true of white, affluent children who are more likely to have Internet access than poor African American or Hispanic students (Office of the Press

Secretary, 2000). Equal access is a big problem; not all children will have it, but they will need it to fully participate in today's information-age society.

The very ugly side of Internet usage includes viruses, security concerns, privacy violations, pornography, dangerous chat rooms, and pedophilia. The last problem listed is the worst—when pedophiles seduce children online and arrange to meet them. In some cases, children have been molested or assaulted by these cyber-stalkers, which makes computer chat rooms a very dangerous place for children to visit. Miles (1997) emphasizes that children must be taught safe, responsible ways to use the Internet. Children should be made aware of the possible dangers lurking in chat rooms and Web sites.

Learning Styles

Learning styles may be referred to as the preferred strategy a person uses to process data. This definition assumes an understanding that individuals respond to information in different ways. A person's prior learning, beliefs, culture, experience, and personal preferences and various socioemotional and psychophysiological factors interact to characterize consistent strategies that a person uses to process information; to construct meanings; to facilitate learning in a particular setting; to perceive, process, and remember information; and to solve problems (Reiff, 1992). Being aware of learning styles can improve achievement; and it can help teachers in becoming more sensitive to learner's needs, providing more individualized instruction, and anticipating effective pedagogy. The premise is that students can successfully master curriculum using strategies and methods that complement the way each student learns.

Dunn (1999) identified various elements that can affect the way a person learns difficult material. He organized it into five different categories:

1. Reaction to the classroom environment preferences for temperature, lighting, sound, and seating
2. Emotional characteristics such as levels of motivation persistence and responsibility
3. Social preferences such as studying alone or with others
4. Physiological characteristics such as perceptual strengths, best time of the day
5. Global vs. analytic processing determined by correlation among sound light design, social preferences, and intake (pp. 1–2)

Increased interest in learning styles has stimulated a demand for reliable learning styles assessments and inventories. Knowing a student's learning style can provide valuable information that could help a teacher to match that student's learning style with the most effective teaching technique, strategy, or pedagogy.

Magnet Schools

Magnet schools are a concept, borrowed from magnetism, which envisions superior schools that offer such innovative, specialized, and inviting instructional approaches that—like a huge magnet—they will attract a cross section of students across all racial, socioeconomic, and ethnic backgrounds.

In the late 1970s, a judge ordered mandatory busing to achieve racial balance in segregated school districts. Magnet schools were spawned in the aftermath of that decision in order to avoid the political fallout associated with busing. The schools were created to address the student problem of very few whites being willing to attend black schools. The lure of obtaining a perceived superior education provides the magnetism in the magnet schools concept.

Magnet schools have a variety of appeals: a specialized thematic, holistic core curriculum; a perception of excellence and orderliness; an enthusiastic, committed faculty; motivated students; involved parents; implementation and adoptions of more educational reforms and innovations; autonomy that allows them to focus more on student outcomes (Inger, 1991).

Magnet schools are criticized as being elitist, engaging in institutional "creaming"—they skim the cream of the academic crop, effectively robbing non-magnet schools of role models. The high selectivity and limited admission of magnet schools offer status to all involved. Students may feel they are the best of the best. One cause for concern is that magnet schools cost more than most non-magnet schools. They siphon off scarce resources for the few, leaving the burden of that depletion on the many. Another concern is that a very small number of magnet schools, even if they were to achieve racial balance, would not be enough to achieve desegregation in a school district (Warren, 1978). An important concern is that not all parents have the educational savvy to make informed choices for their children.

The magnet schools concept is excellent, and it could be very effective if all schools were magnet schools that generated enthusiasm among faculty, motivated students, and offered a superior curriculum. Paradoxically, the magnets schools concept is counter to the notion of quality education for all. Although in many cases, magnet schools have brought school districts into compliance with court-ordered desegregation, they have effectively segregated the best students from average and low-performing students. Many debate the effectiveness of magnet schools. Research indicates that they are effective overall; but like most schools, some are extemporary and some are not. The quality varies on a continuum. For example, the Humanities and Communication Magnet Program at Eastern School offers a curriculum featuring rigorous writing courses, a traditional curriculum, and special events such as mock trials. The program also offers mass media classes in which students produce a game show, deejay at a radio station, and host a talk show.

Mainstreaming

Mainstreaming, in education, is the practice of teaching children with special needs and disabilities in regular classrooms all or part of their day, to the fullest extent possible. The interest in mainstreaming gained momentum with the Civil Rights movement, which stressed the rights of the individual (Columbia University, 1995). Before 1975, children with disabilities had to show enough improvement or ability to meet the expectations of a regular classroom before they were mainstreamed. The Education for All Handicapped Children Act (1975) mandated that all states provide a free, appropriate education for every child between the ages of 3 and 21, regardless of disability, in the least restrictive environment. The children were no longer required to show any evidence of ability to meet expectations. On the contrary, teachers and other resource people were responsible for making sure the school was meeting the child's needs.

Mastery Teaching

Mastery teaching is a popular, research-based instruction model developed by Madeline Hunter in 1981–1982. The Hunter model is based on ascertaining the best practices of the most effective teachers and using this information to delineate a model of instruction that is practical and useful. Hunter (1994) acknowledges that her model is based on techniques that teachers are already using, and that her critics say these techniques are just common sense (Meador, 1993). However, the benefit is that she has labeled the techniques and explained the underlying psychological theory of why these techniques work. Hunter's model is prescriptive in that it outlines a way to teach in a conscious and deliberate fashion to increase student learning. She believes that teachers can become master teachers using the strategies she has delineated.

In the first step of her instructional plan, Hunter introduces the notion of "set." It seems to be the same concept as "ready, set, go" that is used in racing. Set implies getting students ready to learn, which may require a review of prerequisite knowledge. Anticipatory set helps students get motivated for the instructional activities that are to follow. Hunter says this set should be designed within the context of the instructional objectives. The objectives are explained to the students to increase the effectiveness of the lesson. The objectives and the content should be meaningful and relevant to maximize student participation, interest, and learning. The input and modeling step of Hunter's model stresses that the teacher should model what she plans to teach, using effective demonstration and instructional strategy. To test the effectiveness of the instruction, it is important for the teacher to check for understanding and to provide guided practice.

Montessori Method

Dr. Maria Montessori (1870–1952), an Italian educator, physician, and prolific writer, founded the Montessori method of educating children in 1907. Her method, designed to serve disadvantaged children, was based on the premise that children learn better through discovery—by using their senses and pursuing their interests in an environment that offers choice. The Montessori method differs radically from traditional educational methods. The method employs systematic observation techniques that facilitate the learning of difficult concepts across subject areas. Montessori symbolizes a holistic approach to educating the child, focusing on character development, decision making, fostering autonomy, and caring for others.

Maria Montessori's new approach for educating young children was revolutionary. She envisioned young children as capable of learning advanced concepts if they were allowed to work at their own pace, given the appropriate environment and materials, and guided by a skilled directress (teacher). Montessori believed that if the environment were prepared to meet all of their needs, the children would find answers for themselves through exploration and creative pursuit, and they would learn to love learning. The Montessori environment is arranged according to subjects such as math, art, geography, and science. Children are free to move from one area to the next at their own pace. The lessons are well planned and make use of a variety of developmentally appropriate manipulatives. Children are allowed to work at any one activity as long as they want; the choice is theirs. Unlike traditional classrooms, which have to contend with numerous interruptions throughout the day and discrete periods of instructional time for each subject, the Montessori day is scheduled with either one or two long blocks of uninterrupted time. I believe this block-of-time feature is a major strength of the Montessori program. Children develop longer attention spans and a respect for concentration as they learn to persevere and follow through.

The following are important principles of the Montessori method:

1. Children are unique individuals and different from adults.
2. Children are exceptionally capable of learning from their environment.
3. Early childhood is a critical period of intellectual growth during which latent learning becomes conscious learning.
4. Children have a need for purposeful work, and they love doing work for its own sake; they are intrinsically motivated to work.

Montessori materials are designed to accommodate student's needs at each stage of growth. Michael Olaf (2001) offers a variety of Montessori materials online. The *BC Parent News Magazine* (2001) outlines the two curriculums usually found in Montessori schools: a primary curriculum and an elementary curriculum. The elementary curriculum is built on the foundation of the primary, which typically features practical life exercises, sensorial or sensory activities, language exercises, math, and cultural exercises.

A major concern that continues to plague Montessori schooling is whether children who have attended Montessori schools will have difficulty making the transition to traditional schools. Many traditional schools do not offer the autonomy, rigor, and instructional style of Montessori. Despite these concerns, the Montessori method has remained popular for almost 100 years. Research shows some evidence that children who have attended Montessori schools outperform their peers in traditional schools. In some cases, even children who have attended only Montessori preschool may outperform children at higher grade levels (Northwest Regional Education Laboratory, 2001). The success of Montessori schooling generates some compelling questions. Will the children who go into traditional settings lose their Montessori edge? Why aren't some of the successful aspects of Montessori schools more widely used in traditional schools? I think these questions and their answers will continue to fuel debates, but the Montessori method will remain popular for many years to come.

Motivation Theory

Motivation arouses, sustains, and directs behavior to satisfy a need or attain a goal. This definition summarizes the variety of definitions found in motivation literature. Many forces and factors influence motivation: attitude, interests, anxiety, intentions, aspirations, and locus of control (the location of cause and control of our behavior).

If we attribute the causes of our behavior and the responsibility for our fate to ourselves, we are thought to have an internal locus of control. If we attribute the cause of and the responsibility for our behavior to someone or something else, we are thought to have an external locus of control (Rotter, 1966). These sources of motivation affect the way a student is motivated. Usually those with an internal locus of control are intrinsically motivated; that is, they engage in an activity for its own sake and nothing else except the enjoyment and personal satisfaction they derive from it. Students with an external locus are usually extrinsically motivated; they are motivated by some external reward or punishment to participate in the activity. Rewards can be praise, stickers, candy, certificates, and so forth (Lepper, 1988).

Why do people do what they do when they do it? The quest for the answer to this question has inspired various theoretical views of what motivates people. Four important views are behavioral, cognitive, humanistic, and social cognitive. Skinner (1953), who offered a behaviorist view and a stimulus-response model, suggests that consequences determine and maintain behavior. Jerome Bruner (1961) proposed discovery learning as a cognitive view of motivation, through which feelings of accomplishment and self-reward can be an intrinsic form of motivation. Maslow (1970) presented a needs-oriented, humanistic view of motivation that identified a sequence of basic survival needs and growth needs that would have to be satisfied before a person could become self-actualized. Bandura (1986) offered a social-cognitive perspective, proposing that learning by observing was a motivator of behavior.

Some distinct types of motivation are achievement motivation, reading motivation, growth motivation, student motivation, teacher motivation, and motivation to learn. Examples of manifestations of these motivations (or lack of motivation) include teacher burnout, fear of success, self-control, self-motivation, and unmotivated students. The last example is important, because technically there is no "unmotivated" student. Students are motivated. They just might not be motivated to do what we want them to do in the traditional academic setting. Various motivational techniques including incentives, performance contracts, and educational strategies are used in attempting to motivate the unmotivated student to learn.

Multicultural Education

The winds of change were gathering strength as the Civil Rights movement of the 1960s gained momentum. In its wake, change was evident in the contentious multicultural education reform movement that swept the country. Eliminating discrimination was one of the primary goals of the 1960s (Banks & Banks, 1993). Educational institutions were faced with demands to recognize and respond to the cultural needs and rich histories of diverse groups. Burnett (1998) aptly describes multicultural education as a reaction to the tendency to force all groups into America's "melting pot," as it was fondly referred to years ago. Today the far-reaching concept of depicting America as a salad bowl seems to be a more accurate conceptualization of American culture.

There are a variety of definitions and conceptualizations of multicultural education because it means different things to different people. Burnett (1998) suggests that rather than defining multicultural education, using a typology or a framework for thinking about it might help to clarify its meaning. A broad framework can assimilate the various definitions provided by experts in the field. Definitions are determined by their purpose or focus. Burnett (1998) divides multicultural programs into three categories based on emphasis: content-oriented programs that seek to include content about different groups; student-oriented programs that try to address the academic needs of students (particularly African American, Latino or Mexican American, and Native American students); and socially oriented programs that seek to reform schooling, reduce racial bias, and increase racial and cultural tolerance.

The contentious hue of multiculturalism is painted by the fear, racism, and misperceptions that permeated the Civil Rights movements. Whites feared that multicultural education would destroy or diminish their culture and history. Blacks adamantly expressed their anger over and intolerance of the eurocentric bias that had dominated American textbooks and curriculum for decades. Opponents feared that multiculturalism was divisive and would further divide an already divided country. Proponents advocated real change, not just a band-aid on deficient curriculum and educational approach. Despite much controversy, the winds of change spawned by the turbulence of the 1960s Civil Rights movement had a significant impact on education.

The response to urgent demands to change was manifest in the rush to develop multicultural texts, courses, curriculums, studies, articles, and resources. Multicultural resources include diversity training videos, flags, calendars, posters, songs, and books. Multiculturalism has changed the face of characters appearing in children's books, textbooks posters, toys, and so on to include a variety of colors, shapes, and distinctions to represent the various microcultures found in the United States. Further evidence of change is also found in changes to assessment tests. Test makers have revised tests in attempts to reduce cultural bias, and they have added color to pictures of people to symbolize diversity. More change is evident as the concept of multicultural education continues to evolve. Perhaps the winds of change will touch all of us and increase our ability to recognize, accept, and celebrate our differences.

Multiple Intelligences

The genesis of IQ testing dates back to 1904, when Alfred Binet was commissioned by the French minister of public education to design an instrument that would identify children with a need for special education. Binet's test was designed to identify cognitive or intellectual skills that a child needed to be successful in school. Howard Gardner's theory of multiple intelligences (1983) departs from the traditional concept of intelligence to offer a fresh, multidimensional approach to the definition and assessment of human intelligence. Gardner's theory defines intelligence as a set of skills, talents, and abilities that individually or collectively enhance human productivity. Others have alluded to the multidimensionality of intelligence (Spearman, 1927; Thurstone, 1938), but none have developed the theory to Gardner's level of sophistication. Critics of Gardner's theory propose that the seven intelligences are not new, that they in fact resemble the cognitive-style constructs and IQ factors identified in other theories of intelligence (Morgan, 1992).

Multiple intelligences (MI) theory proposes that humans possess several autonomous intelligences in varying degrees and configurations. In the multiple intelligences context, intelligences refer to problem-solving ability and the ability to create products that are valued in one or more cultural settings (Gardner & Hatch, 1989). Gardner presents seven intelligences and is entertaining the possible existence of an eighth. According to Gardner, the following intelligences have both a biological and a cultural basis:

1. Logical mathematical intelligence consists of deductive reasoning, logical thinking, and pattern detection.
2. Linguistic intelligence suggests a mastery of language that facilitates memory and expression.
3. Spatial intelligence involves the ability to create and manipulate mental images as a process of problem solving, even in the visually impaired.
4. Musical intelligence involves a capacity to compose and recognize musical tones, pitch, and rhythms.
5. Bodily kinesthetic intelligence is the ability to control and coordinate one's body movements.
6. Interpersonal intelligence involves the ability to understand one's own feelings, intentions, and motivations.
7. Intrapersonal intelligence refers to knowing and understanding oneself—feelings, thoughts, needs, and abilities.
8. The eighth intelligence, the naturalist, gives one the ability to discriminate between living things and be sensitive to the wonders of nature.

The benefits of a theory that respects the multidimensionality of intelligence are many. For one, it allows people to be smart in more ways than one. It also encourages teachers to recognize and develop latent or unrecognized talents and abilities in children. Awarenesses created from such a theory help students attach value to their talents, skills, and abilities that are typically not recognized by traditional educational assessment measures. MI theory invites schools to broaden their curriculum to include multiple intelligences in their lessons, activities, and assessment techniques. Gardner's theory offers parents an opportunity to participate in the recognition and development of their child's talents and abilities. Current research indicates that the theory of multiple intelligences has become a key component in academic success. Multiple intelligences is still fuzzy as a construct. The theory will benefit from further research and dialogue.

Outcome-Based Education

Outcome-based education (OBE) began in the 1950s. It was heavily influenced by Skinner's (1953) behavioral modification theory and Benjamin Bloom's (1956) Taxonomy of Instructional Objectives, particularly in the affective (feelings) domain. Proponents of outcome-based learning associate affective skills with higher-level learning. Schools that embrace outcome-based learning usually direct all school activities and functions toward meeting mastery expectations and specific learning outcomes.

In outcome-based education, students are not required to earn traditional high school credits or letter grades. Instead, they must meet specific learning outcomes that are usually feelings-based and subjective. An important principle of outcome-based education is the mandate for a 100 percent success rate for each school. All students must achieve mastery. A success rate of 100 percent sounds like a noble goal, but it is really a source of serious contention. Insisting on a 100 percent success rate increases the probability that accelerated students may be restricted and held back until slower students catch up. A major concern of opponents is that slower students may not be able to meet the learning outcomes—so educators may be forced to lower the bar, and lower it again until the slower students achieve the mastery required by outcome-based education (Williams, 1994).

OBE also requires that all learning activity be specifically associated with the learning outcomes. The exit outcomes should be clearly defined. Faculty and staff are directed to use whatever means and resources necessary to guarantee student success. Lowering the bar for slow students may be the reason Tancredo (1994) feels that outcome-based education degrades students learning. Other opponents of OBE question the rigor and fairness of its philosophy. They believe that OBE learning outcomes appear to relate to student attitudes and beliefs rather than to knowledge and information required. Despite the criticisms, OBE often produces students who do achieve mastery and have long-lasting results.

Psychological Schools of Thought

The Age of Enlightenment or Reason marks the advent of our intellectual awakening. It was a time when humankind abandoned the fear, mysticism, and ignorance that had limited their thinking and began to engage in deep thought and wondrous discoveries. Learning theories are rooted in the thoughts of great thinkers of the past. These thinkers expressed their thoughts in writing and in presentations. Others read or pondered these thoughts, discussing and judging them. When the work of great thinkers was acknowledged and recognized, young students would clamor to study under these master thinkers. Many of the young scholars sought to contribute their own thoughts, often building on those of their mentor, with hopes of expanding the current knowledge in that area.

New thinking gradually phased out the old thinking, giving way to new schools of thought in which a particular psychological or philosophical viewpoint dominated. These schools of thought had a profound influence on shaping education and generating the contemporary learning theories of today.

The following schools of thought are presented in order of occurrence to illuminate the development of thinking and the evolution of contemporary learning theories. Each school of thought is represented by the time period of the dominant theorist(s), and the basic tenets and principles of the thinking for that school of thought. Schools of thought use the suffix *-ism* to indicate that it is a distinctive theory, system of principles, or set of beliefs about a particular topic.

Rationalism (René Descartes, 1596–1650)
- Knowledge is gained from reasoning.
- There is a distinction between the mind and body.
- Ideas are a product of the workings of the mind. The senses aren't necessary; one can doubt sensory experiences.
- Embraced a theory of inquiry via doubt. By doubting in a deductive manner, going from general ideas to specific ideas, Descartes was able to derive conclusions that resisted doubt. He was able to prove God's existence and his own using doubt. He said people could not doubt their existence as thinking human beings. He based that on his Latin dictum, *cogito, ergo sum*—"I think, therefore I am" (Wozniak, 1996).
- Being a mathematician, Descartes was disturbed that philosophy was so uncertain, unlike the preciseness of mathematics. He believed it was his task in life to rescue human knowledge from the skepticism that accompanies uncertainty. He developed a plan for applying mathematical principles to philosophical ideas to create more certainty about them.

Empiricism (John Locke, 1632–1704)
- Reflected on origins of human knowledge and concluded that our knowledge is derived from experiences (Kemerling, 1996).
- Believed that ideas in the mind had to come through the senses, and that ideas were not innate because man is born with a tabula rasa, or blank slate. Knowledge is gained as each experience from the external world (sight, sound taste) is "recorded" on the blank tablet of the mind.

Structuralism (Edward Titchener, 1867–1927)
- Influenced learning by introducing the experimental method and the ideas of associationism.
- Used introspection as the experimental method to examine the structure of consciousness or mental processes. Self-analyzed the mental processes by careful observation to determine the structure or basic building blocks. The intent was to ignore the stimulus or its name, such as "chair" and focus only on describing the mental experience.
- Believed the mind is comprised of ideas associated with other ideas, and that this association must be broken down into a single idea to understand what it is.
- Sought to study the brain by breaking it down into its elementary parts, just as a chemist breaks down complex substances (Benjafield, 1996).

Functionalism (John Dewey, 1859–1952)
- A reaction to structuralism that focused on the way mental processes help humans adapt to their environment.

- It was a practical theory that had tremendous influence on American education.
- Incorporates the thinking of William James, but the functionalist movement was marked by Dewey's rejection of the structuralist theory of breaking mental processes down into parts. Dewey argued that these processes should be viewed holistically.
- Believed that stimulus and responses should not be broken down into discrete parts, and that the stimulus-response phenomena are not automatic; takes a person's goals and intent into consideration. The goal or intent actually elicits a response (Campbell, Davis, Dunder, Stoffel, & Tarsoly, 2000).
- Observed how mental processes worked, what they did, and how they varied as environmental conditions varied, to help a person adapt.
- Believed that the way a person acts in the environment is the way they learn. Believed that psychology should be applied to everyday life.
- Developed the laboratory school in 1886, which gave birth to pragmatism, or basing the curriculum on everyday life, as a school of thought. In the Dewey school, children learned experientially, or from hands-on experiences using a scientifically tested curriculum. Dewey strived for a balance between philosophy and natural science (Hickman, 1996).
- Dewey's ideas had a marked influence on education, to the extent that he was identified as a progressivist.
- Though Dewey did not totally agree with progressivism, some of his thoughts were espoused by the progressivist movement:

  - ▲ Education should be everyday life and not a preparation for making a living.
  - ▲ Children should be taught at a developmentally appropriate level that considers their interests.
  - ▲ Children should learn through problem solving, but advanced analytical methods should be saved for the later years of their education.
  - ▲ Children should have some control over what they are to learn, but not necessarily be free to study whatever they want to study.
  - ▲ Curriculum content should be meaningful, relevant, and preferably in a context of the child's choosing.

Connectionism (Edward L. Thorndike, 1874–1949)

- Work with animals in a puzzle box was a major contribution to psychology.
- Postulated that learning involves connections between a stimulus and a response.
- Did experiment with cat in a puzzle box; the cat had to figure out by trial and error how to get out of the box (pushing a button, pulling a string, etc.).

- Results of this experiment provided the foundation of Thorndike's famous law of effect, in which he postulated that stimulus-response sequences that are followed by a pleasurable response or a satisfying state of affairs are likely to be repeated. Stimulus-response sequences that are followed by pain or an annoying state of affairs are "stamped out" and are not likely to be repeated (Reinemeyer, 1996).
- Theory includes two principles that are relative to education, the law of readiness and associative shifting.

Behaviorism (John B. Watson, 1878–1958)

- Founder of behaviorism, an objective psychology that borrows heavily from Pavlov's classical conditioning and rejects the notions of introspection, functionalism, and so on, as being archaic, unscientific, and unreliable.
- Watson believed that human behavior should be studied in a manner that allows the researcher to predict and control those behaviors.
- Believed that the study of psychology should be scientific and that data or phenomena should be observable and measurable.
- Behaviorism was considered anti-mentalism because it reduced the concept of thinking as an implicit response. According to Watson, thinking was merely talking to oneself. He later retracted that assertion (Watson, 1996).
- Conducted the "Little Albert" experiment to demonstrate that fear could be conditional in children. Over several trials, Watson presented a white rat—simultaneously with a loud gong sound—to a boy named Little Albert. Initially Little Albert did not fear the rat; but after the experiment, he did. In fact, his fear was generalized to other white, fuzzy objects.
- Behaviorism contends that human behavior can be explained as just a relationship between a stimulus and a response, and learned behavior is just a conditioned response.

Associationism (Edwin R. Guthrie, 1886–1959)

- Rejected connectionism and the use of rewards and punishments in favor of a theory of learning based on contiguity and association. Agreed that a study of behavior must be based on observation.
- Contiguity—whatever behavioral response is performed in a given situation, the same behavior is likely to occur in a recurrence of that situation (Guthrie, 1952).
- Contends that all learning is simply a result of a stimulus-response association, where there is close pairing of the stimulus and the response.
- Believed in one-trial learning in which the behavior gains strength in the first pairing with a response.
- Believed a habit was a behavioral response to a cue, and to change that behavior it would be necessary to first find the cue and then associate another behavior with that cue (sidetracking). It is easier to

sidetrack than to change a habit (Peterson, 1996).

- Offered three methods for changing habits—threshold method, fatigue method, and incompatible response.

Cognitivism (Noam Chomsky, 1928– ; Jerome Bruner, 1915–)

- Chomsky was responsible for a resurgence of interest in mental processes such as attention, memory, imagery, and so on. He argued that behaviorist theory could not explain the complexities of language and that behaviorism was lacking in scientific content (Crabtree, 1996).
- Bruner co-founded cognitive psychology with George Miller in 1956. Miller is known for his work on information processing theory (Campbell et al., 2000).
- Bruner showed evidence that mental processes were observable and measurable.
- Bruner developed a cognitive learning theory of categorization. He proposed that people think and interpret the world in categories, using a coding system that arranges related categories into a hierarchy that inductively goes from the specific to the general.

Constructivism (Bruner, 1915–)

- Contends that learning is an active process, and educators should help children construct their own meaning, ideas, and concepts based on knowledge gained from their past experiences.
- Believes the teacher should act as a facilitator, translating information to be learned in a developmentally appropriate format that is informed by the learner's current understandings.
- Advocates discovery learning, through which students discover principles for themselves, and the teacher uses guided facilitation to maintain the integrity of the students' independent efforts to construct knowledge.
- Believes in a spiral curriculum that reintroduces key concepts again and again in higher grades, so that children can build on what they have learned previously and expand their knowledge (Kearsley, 2001).
- Bruner thinks the learning environment should be structured to provide and encourage opportunities to construct knowledge and to build understanding.
- Constructivism is the most current learning theory. Educators are encouraged to release the grip the behaviorists have had on instruction and learning over the past several decades. Teachers are encouraged to allow students time to reflect and think about information rather than give them the answers right away. Teachers should view mistakes as an opportunity to learn and a natural part of the learning process. (Behaviorists believe mistakes should be punished.) Teachers are also encouraged to give students the opportunity to reflect on and assess their own academic performance. If children are

to learn to construct knowledge, the teacher must be willing to assume the role of facilitator and resist the urge to make their instruction teacher-centered (Tella, 1996).

School Vouchers

The specter of school vouchers was summoned as a long-awaited solution to the apparent academic deficit of the American public school system. It arrived shrouded in contention, ablaze with fiery political rhetoric and embroiled in heated political debate. Ideally, the voucher program would subsidize tuition costs for public schoolchildren who wish to go to private schools and for children who are already in private schools. Friedman (2000) suggests that vouchers would empower parents and students by giving them options. Effectively, vouchers would create a new market of paying customers that could take their child someplace else if their school is performing poorly. Schools would have to improve their performance, or risk having to close their doors due to low enrollments. Friedman is a Nobel Prize winning economist. Understandably, he believes that the free market competition generated by choice will improve education. He predicts that this new market of education consumers would attract enterprising entrepreneurs and encourage them to come up with innovative methods of delivering education.

The voucher system is based on the assumption that public schools are deficient—an assumption that voucher opponents argue has not been scientifically proven. Many believe that urban schools offer an education inferior to that offered by private schools. This stance is particularly significant for African American and Mexican American children, who usually comprise the bulk of urban schools' student population and are most likely to be affected by any deficiencies in instruction. Kurt Schmoke (1999) contends that the voucher program is good for African American children. He believes that a voucher program offers accountability and excellence. Vouchers are strongly supported by the Religious Right political movement. According to People for the American Way (2001), the Religious Right group is merely seeking government funding for sectarian schools and religious instruction.

The voices of voucher opposition have called the voucher program elitist and racist (Schmoke, 1999). Many opponents believe that a voucher by any other name, be it tax credits or tuition scholarships, is still a scheme to lighten the coffers of urban schools that are already in financial crisis. They acknowledge that although vouchers may benefit a few students, many students left behind would have to endure inadequate academic conditions as a result. Others argue that private schools are less responsive to the special needs of children and, considering they hand-pick their students, they are less likely to pick children with disabilities or other special needs. There is intense debate about the effectiveness of vouchers. Many opponents believe vouchers have a minimal effect on academic achievement (People for the American Way, 2001). The biggest argument is that vouchers tend to benefit affluent families more than the low-income families for which they are intended. Only one fourth of voucher children in private schools come from public schools (National Education Association and American Federation of Teachers, 1998–1999).

The voucher proposal has been so political that it is difficult to know which side is the right side. The voucher dilemma has been blamed on teachers unions, property tax laws, and so on. The arguments suggest to me that vouchers and choice have become synonymous—that you cannot have one without the other. This is an erroneous assumption. Many appear to be arguing for vouchers when they are truly arguing for choice. Other viable alternatives may offer choice without the ill effects of vouchers. The National Education Association and the American Federation of Teachers (1998–1999) suggest implementing a program like Success For All or Goals 2000 as an alternative.

Self-Regulation

The shift from teacher-centered education to more learner-centered education has generated significant interest in finding ways to encourage students to become more self-regulated. Research on self-regulation has increased exponentially in recent years. It has produced numerous definitions of self-regulation, reflecting a variety of theoretical perspectives. Careful examination of the literature reveals considerable overlap in definitions. A summary of those definitions might define self-regulation as a student's willingness and ability to effectively manage or direct their learning using appropriate strategies and attitudes that help them to sustain goal-directed behaviors and to seek assistance when necessary. The proliferation of variant definitions underscores the complexity of self-regulation.

Schunk (1996) integrates cognitive, social, behavioral, and developmental perspectives in explaining self-regulation. The following characterizations of the different perspectives comprising self-regulation illuminate this integration. Cognitively, the development of intellect moves the student from a more external, other-regulation to an internal self-regulation (Dixon-Krauss, 1996). Cognitive changes develop over time, increasing the student's ability to make more mature intellectual decisions. Self-efficacy, or the student's positive belief about his or her abilities to perform tasks and reach goals, is critical to effective self-regulation (Bandura, 1986). Social interaction is crucial for effective self-regulation. Students must know when to ask for assistance and be willing to ask for and accept help. Developmentally, the capacity for self-regulation increases as the student develops the resources to motivate the self and to sustain appropriate behaviors until a goal developed by the self is attained. The student's ability to process information increases over time. The student progressively becomes more adept at monitoring the self and the cognitive processes that foster self-monitoring. Behaviorally, the gradual acquisition of appropriate study strategies and attitudes provide the nuts and bolts of self-regulatory behavior. Once a student has selected and employed self-regulatory behaviors and capacities, the student must also actively participate in evaluating the effectiveness of his or her performance and be willing to make changes when necessary.

Several subprocesses of self-regulation are found in the literature. The following subprocesses reflect the cognitive, behavioral, social, and developmental perspectives or views of self-regulation described by Schunk (1996). The behavioral or reinforcement view is associated with self-monitoring, self-instruction, and self-reinforcement. The developmental view looks at self-monitoring (private speech), self-instruction, self-verbalization, and verbal self-reinforcement. The cognitive or information processing view emphasizes self-monitoring, self-judging, and self-reaction. The social view considers self-reaction, self-judgment, and self-observation or self-evaluation (Bandura, 1986; Zimmerman, 1989; Schunk, 1996). Some subprocesses of self-regulation may be a combination of views, or the same subprocesses may be viewed differently according to perspective. Subprocesses that may be a combination of views are self-pacing, self-motivation, and self-efficacy (Bandura, 1982; Zimmerman & Martinez-Pons, 1990).

The Self-Regulation Inventory (SRI) is a measure of self-regulation (Orange, 1999). The SRI addresses the multidimensionality of self-regulation through the integration of cognitive, social, behavioral, and developmental perspectives of self-regulation proposed by Schunk (1996).

Situated Learning

Lev Vygotsky's sociocultural theory, which suggests that children's thinking is influenced by their social and cultural interactions, laid the foundation for situated learning. Traditional education has ignored the social character of learning. The learner is expected to learn isolated facts and information individually.

Lave and Wenger (1991) suggest that we rethink the concept of learning and see it as the reception of information and facts. They believe social interaction is a major component of situated learning. Their theory is concerned with where learning takes place, or is situated. These authors also propose that learning is a process of coparticipation that at first is legitimately peripheral, but increases gradually in the level of engagement and complexity as the learner gains knowledge. In other words, learners start as novice participants; as they gain skill and mastery, they become more expert. Through involvement in everyday activities, they gradually become full participants in the sociocultural practices of their community. Finally, they are transformed from novice to expert and from newcomer to old-timer. Lave and Wenger (1991) believe that "learning is a process that takes place in a participation framework, not in an individual mind" (p. 15).

The legitimate peripheral participation process (situated learning) assumes that learners learn unconsciously, rather than deliberately, in their efforts to become fully participating members of their community and to assimilate the values, knowledge, and beliefs of their culture. Two principles with important implications for education have emerged from this theory: (1) knowledge should be presented in authentic settings involving authentic applications and activities; and (2) learning should be a social, collaborative enterprise.

Social Learning

Bandura (1977) conceptualized a social learning theory (also known as social cognitive learning) that explained learning as observing others or observational learning. His theory extended beyond the stimulus-response theories of the behaviorists to include cognitive factors such as attention, beliefs, memory, self-perceptions, and self-efficacy or one's belief about their own capabilities. Social learning theory bridges behaviorism and cognitivism with notions of observational learning, modeling other's behavior, vicarious reward, and vicarious punishment.

Social learning involves two major steps, supported by four processes of observational learning. Step one is acquisition, and step two is performance. A distinction is made between acquisition and performance because a person can acquire a behavior and may not perform it right away, but may wait until later to perform it. The four subprocesses of social learning are attention and retention, which are necessary for acquisition; and production and motivation, which are necessary for performance (Schunk, 2000). For example, suppose two teenagers are attending a popular concert and dance. Everyone is excited about the new dance that one of the groups is teaching to the audience. The two teenagers watch the dance steps intently (attention). They try to memorize the dance steps (retention). After watching for a while, they think they know the steps well enough to try the dance. They have acquired the necessary behavior. Both teens are mentally and physically capable of imitating the dancers in producing the act (production). One teenager is excited and eager to practice the dance (motivation), so she begins to perform the dance with the group. The other teenager has acquired the dance steps but is not ready to perform them. He will not perform them until he goes home to practice. It is difficult to know if he has learned by observing until he performs the dance at home.

Social learning theory embraces three basic principles:

- An observer is more likely to model observed behavior if the model has characteristics, such as looks and talent, that the observer admires. For example, when Jacqueline Kennedy Onassis was first lady, many people rushed to copy her style, her hairdo, her pillbox hats, and her fuzzy suits.
- An observer is likely to model the observed behavior if it results in outcomes that are valued or rewarded (vicarious reinforcement or reward). For example, when a person sees another person win big on a lottery ticket, they are more likely to buy a lottery ticket.
- An observer is less likely to model behavior if it is punished (vicarious punishment). For example, a person is observing looters stealing from stores during a riot. Just when she is about steal something, she sees a group of police officers arrive and arrest some of the looters. She is less likely to take something after seeing what happened to the others (vicarious punishment).

Several factors may influence the likelihood that an observer will model a behavior. The observer's developmental level and attention span are important factors. If a young child is an observer, she might not be able to acquire or perform the modeling behavior. The status and prestige of the model are also significant. This is evident in many commercials. A popular slogan is "I want to be like Mike," referring to Michael Jordan, the famous basketball player. If a model is similar to the observer, the observer is more likely to imitate the model's behavior. In high schools across the country, teenagers readily imitate the latest styles in clothing, hair, language, and so on. The trendsetters for these styles are usually other teenagers who are similar to them.

Whole Language

The meaning of whole language depends on the perspective taken. Some view it as an approach to teaching literacy skills, and others believe it is a philosophy. The development of the whole language philosophy began in the 1970s with Goodman's (1969) work in applied psycholinguistics. Weaver (1990) defines the whole-language philosophy as a belief system about the nature of learning and how it can be fostered in classrooms and schools. It is not an approach, although some kinds of activities can reasonably be characterized as whole language because they are in agreement with this philosophy. In whole language, language is kept whole, not fragmented into "skills." Literacy skills and strategies are developed in the context of authentic literacy events, while reading and writing experiences permeate the whole curriculum. Learning within the classroom is integrated within the whole life of the learner.

Proponents of whole language believe that children should learn to read without direct instruction, similar to the way they acquired language. In a typical whole-language program, children read and write daily in the context of meaningful literacy activities. They use cues from print, such as configuration clues and context clues, to decode words. They are taught to recognize whole words by memorizing them one word at a time. Whole language is not like the phonics approach, in which children learn syllables and phonetic word-attack skills that allow them to decode unfamiliar words. Reading, oral, and written language are considered as a whole rather than as separate skills. Whole language is most effective when children are allowed to learn by doing. That is, they learn by reading—preferably without fear, ridicule, embarrassment, or shame.

The whole-language instruction program has come under fire and gained notoriety as one of the opponents in the famed "reading wars." Opponents are harshly critical of the whole-language program. Williams (1994) refers to whole language as a dressed-up version of the obsolete, discredited look-say technique of reading. Some parents and educators are concerned that teachers do not correct grammar and spelling in the whole-language program. Their worst fears are that this practice will spawn a generation of poor spellers and illiterates. Overall, whole language is a good idea; but the call for a balance of whole language and phonics has echoed through the literature in recent years. Most educators and parents want to see the end of the reading wars.

Epilogue

I recall a children's book titled *What Did You Bring Me?* (Kuskin, 1973). It is the story of Edwina Mouse, who loved things. Whenever one of her parents returned home, Edwina first said "Hello," and in the next breath, "What did you bring me?" Eventually the house was so full of things that there was very little room for Edwina and her family. "The more things she had, the more things she wanted, until everything in the mouse household had something underneath it, something next to it, and something on top of it" (p. 6).

I recently visited an abandoned alternative school that the school district was using as a storage facility. Schools from around the city sent materials from their abandoned programs: whole kits; used but mostly unused products; lots of manipulatives, workbooks, and books. Everything was delivered to the doorstep of the facility. I was told that on one delivery day, the products were left at the front door in the breezeway and most of the delivery was destroyed by rain. Brand-new, beautiful materials were literally thrown into rooms that were already stacked to the ceiling. The materials lay there untouched for over a year, dead in the sense that children were not using them. They had been sent to the graveyard of abandoned programs to rest in peace. Appalled at such blatant waste, I questioned the reasoning behind it. Why would schools that claim to have little money waste it on programs that they apparently did not want to keep? Perhaps the glamour of a program wears off as soon as a new program appears on the scene. Perhaps schools have a genuine lack of knowledge about the programs or practices appropriate for their educational setting. Unfortunately, they adopt a trial-and-error approach—and the error inevitably generates a lot of waste.

   Schools must be careful not to fall prey to the "Edwina syndrome." They should not welcome anyone and everyone who claims to have the magic pill for school reform or improvement or best practices. It is imperative that they resist the urge to open their wallets and ask, "What did you bring me?" Failure to heed such a warning could result in classroom storage areas brimming over with unused, expensive reform program materials that have lost their luster and appeal, or have been abandoned for the next shiny new program that holds great promise. Requesting evidence of effectiveness and thoroughly researching the progress and reception of the program at sites where the program has been implemented will temper the urge to purchase. Putting the excitement of a new program into a reasonable perspective will encourage consumers of educational products to ask some pertinent questions: Will it improve achievement for students? Will it be accessible to all students? Will there be opportunities for success for all children, regardless of their challenges? Will it deplete resources from other, possibly more effective programs? Will it be a viable product for a long time to come? By seeking appropriate answers to these questions and others like them, educators can avoid the Edwina syndrome and ensure that all program dollars are used effectively.

References

Academy of Orton-Gillingham (1998). Academy of Orton-Gillingham Practioners and Educators [Online]. Available: http://www.ols.net/users/orton/index.htm.

Adler, M. J. (1984). *The Paideia proposal: An educational manifesto.* New York: Collier Books.

American Art Therapy Association, Inc. (1999). Frequently asked questions about art therapy [Online]. Available: http://www.arttherapy.org.

American heritage dictionary of the English language (3rd ed., 1992). Houghton Mifflin. Electronic version licensed from Infosoft International, Inc. All rights reserved.

Ausselin, M. (1999). Balanced Literacy. *Teacher Librarian, 27*(1), 69–70.

Association for Effective Schools (2000). What is effective schools research? [Online]. Available: http://www.mes.org/esr.html.

Ausubel, D. (1960). *The psychology of meaningful verbal learning.* New York: Grune & Stratton.

Bandura, A. (1977). *Social learning theory.* Englewood Cliffs, NJ: Prentice Hall.

Bandura, A. (1982). Self-efficacy in human agency. *American Psychologist, 37,* 122–147.

Bandura, A. (1986). *Social foundations of thought and action: A social cognitive theory.* Englewood Cliffs: NJ: Prentice Hall.

Banikowski, A. K., & Mehring, T. A. (1999). Strategies to enhance memory based on brain research. *Focus on Exceptional Children, 32*(2), 1–16.

Banks, J., & Banks, C. (1993). *Multicultural education: Issues and perspectives.* Needham Heights, MA: Allyn and Bacon.

BC Parent News Magazine (2001, September). Montessori schooling [Online]. Available: http://www.bcparent.com/education/monte.htm.

Bell, M. (1995). From the desk of Max Bell. *TeacherLink, 2*(3), 4.

Benjafield, J. G. (1996). *The developmental point of view.* Needham Heights, MA: Simon & Schuster.

Berreth, D. G. (2000, March 1). Supporting schools as true communities of character. Testimony before the house subcommittee on early childhood, youth, and families [Online]. Available: www.ascd.org/educationnews/pr/early_childhood_testimony.html.

Bloom, B. S., Englehart, M. D., Frost, E. J., Hill, W. H., & Krathwohl, D. R. (1956). *Taxonomy of educational objectives. Handbook I: Cognitive domain.* New York: David McKay.

Board on Teacher Assessment of National Academy of Sciences. (1999, February 3). Assessment and teacher quality. In Colloquium Report [Online]. Available: www.aera.net.

Bruner, J. (1961). The act of discovery. *Harvard Educational Review, 31*(1), 21–32.

Bruner, J. (1967). *On knowing: Essays for the left hand.* Cambridge, MA: Harvard University Press.

Burnett, G. (1998). Varieties of multicultural education: An introduction. *ERIC Clearinghouse on Urban Education* Digest 98 [Online]. Available: http://eric-web.tc.columbia.edu/digests/dig98.html.

Burnett, M. A. (2000–2001, December/January). "One strike and you're out." An analysis of no pass, no play policies. *The High School Journal, 84*(2), 1–6.

Buzan, T. (1993). *The mind map book.* New York: Dutton.

Caine, R., & Caine, G. (1994). *Making connections: Teaching and the human brain.* Boston: Addison-Wesley.

California Teacher Association (1998). Performance anxiety: Who's to blame if students don't measure up? [Online]. *California Education, 2*(9). Available: http://www.cta.org/cal_educator/archive_design1/features/v2i9_performance.html

Cameron, J., & Pierce, W. P. (1994). Reinforcement, reward and intrinsic motivation: A meta-analysis. *Review of Educational Research, 64*(5), 363–423.

Campbell, K., Davis, H., Dunder, R., Stoffel, B., & Tarsoly, S. (2000). Psychological schools of thought [Online]. Available: http://www.webrenovators.com/psych/credits.htm.

Canter, L., & Canter, M. (1992). *Lee Canter's Assertive Discipline: Positive behavior management for today's classroom.* Santa Monica, CA: Lee Canter & Associates.

Cantu, L. (1998, June). Traditional methods of identifying gifted students overlook many. In *Intercultural Development Research Association Newsletter* [Online]. Available: www.idra.org/newlttr/1998/Jun/Linda.

Carroll, B. (1993). Fourth-grade everyday mathematics field test results: Students score high on tests. *TeacherLink, 2*(1), 3.

Chapel Hill Herald (1993, October 15). D.A.R.E. to question. *Chapel Hill Herald,* Forum section.

Character Education Partnership. (2000). [Online]. Available: www. character.org.

Chmelynski, C. (1998). Summer school for meeting higher standards. *Education Digest, 63*(9), 47–50.

Clay, M. (1966). *Emergent reading behaviour.* Unpublished doctoral dissertation, University of Auckland, New Zealand.

Clay, M. (1991). *Reading recovery: A guidebook for teachers in training.*

Columbia University. (1995). *The concise Columbia encyclopedia.* New York: Columbia University Press.

Communities in Schools [Online]. Available: http://www.cisnet.org/index.html.

Conderman, G. (1998). How are we practicing inclusion? *Kappa Delta Phi Record, 34*(2), 52–54.

Cooke, R. (1992). *Legal aspects of no pass, no play in high school extracurricular activities.* Unpublished doctoral dissertation, University of North Carolina.

Core Knowledge Foundation. (1999). About Core Knowledge [Online]. Available: http://www.coreknowledge.org.

Council for Exceptional Children (1989). Delivering Special Education: Statistics and Trends [Online]. ERIC Digest, 463. Publication Sales, 1920 Association Dr., Reston, VA 22091. (ERIC Document Reproduction Service No. ED 308 686.) Available: http://www.askeric.org/plweb-cgi/obtain.pl.

Crabtree, E. (1996). Noam Chomsky [Online]. Available: http://www.muskingum.edu/~psychology/psycweb/history/Chomsky.htm.

Craik, F., & Lockhart, R. (1972). Levels of processing. A framework for memory research. *Journal of Verbal Learning and Verbal Behaviour, 11,* 671–684.

Creative Education Institute (CEI). (1997). *Essential learning systems teacher's manual.* Waco, TX: Author.

Creative Education Institute (CEI). (2000a). Educational resource for math and reading [Online]. Available: http://www.cei-waco.com/companyinfo.cfm.

Creative Education Institute (CEI). (2000b). *SHARE.* Waco, TX: Rutherford Publishing.

Cronbach, L. J. (1960). *Essentials of psychological testing* (2nd ed.). New York: Harper & Row.

Crumpler, L. (1993). Sexual harassment in schools. *NASB Employee Relations Quarterly, 1*(4), 5.

Cunningham, C. (1997). Character education: A general introduction [Online]. Available: http://cuip.uchicago.edu/~cac/chared/intro.htm.

Curwin, R., & Mendler, A. (1998). Zero tolerance. *Phi Delta Kappan, 81*(2), 119–120.

D.A.R.E. America (2000). Suggested response to principles of effectiveness [Online]. Available: http://www.dare.com.

Darling-Hammond, L. (1991). The implications of testing policy for quality and equality. *Phi Delta Kappan, 73,* 220–225.

Davis, K. (1996). Arts magnet draws criticism: School officials vow to address the problems that beset the new Hope Essential Arts program for seventh- and eighth-grade students. *Providence Journal-Bulletin,* D1.

Davis, O. (1996, Winter). No pass, no play and no research: A look into a bare cupboard. *Journal of Curriculum and Supervision, 11,* 107–109.

De La Rosa, D. (1998, April/May). Why alternative education works. *The High School Journal, 81*(4), 268–272.

deCharms, R. (1976). *Enhancing motivation.* New York: Irvington.

DeJong, T., & Van Jooligen, W. R. (1998, Summer). Scientific discovery learning with a computer simulation of conceptual domains. *Review of Educational Research, 68*(2), 179–201.

Delquadri, J., Greenwood, C., Stretton, K., & Hall, R. V. (1983). The peer tutoring game: A classroom procedure for increasing opportunity to respond to spelling performance. *Education and Treatment of Children, 52,* 535–542.

DeRoche, E. F. (2000, September). Leadership for character education programs. *Journal of humanistic counseling, education and development, 39*(1), 41–46.

Dewey, J. (1938). *Experience and education.* New York: MacMillan.

Dillon, B. S. (1998, November/December). SetQuest Interactive. *Book Report, 17*(3), 88.

Dixon-Krauss, L. (1996). Vygotsky's sociohistorical perspective on learning and its application to western literacy instruction. In L. Dixon-Krauss (Ed.), *Vygotsky in the classroom: Mediated literacy instruction and assessment.* White Plains, NY: Longman.

Dunn, R. (1999). How do we teach them if we don't know how they learn? *Teaching Pre-K–8, 29*(7), 50–52.

Edmonds, R. R. (1979a). Effective schools for the urban poor. *Educational Leadership, 37*(1), 15–24.

Edmonds, R. R. (1979b). Some schools work and more can. *Social Policy, 9,* 28–32.

Education Research Network (1999, February/March). *Assessment and Teacher Quality.* Author.

El-Hindi, A. (1998). Beyond classroom boundaries: Constructivist teaching with the Internet, children's literature in the classroom [Online]. Available: http://www.readingonline.org/electronic/RT/Constructivist.html.

Ennett, S. T., Tobler, N. S., & Ringwalt, C. L. (1994, September). How effective is drug abuse resistance education? A meta-analysis of Project D.A.R.E. outcome evaluations. *American Journal of Public Health, 84,* 1394–1401.

Farber, P. (1998). The Edison project scores and stumbles in Boston. *Phi Delta Kappan, 79*(7), 506.

Farius, R., & Tatum, M. (2001, March 24). Charter schools in need of broad support. *San Antonio Express News,* 11B.

Friedman, M. (2000, September 28). Why America needs school vouchers. *Wall Street Journal* [Online]. Available: http://proquest.umi.com/pqdweb?TS=9703276..=1&Sid=1&Idx=3&Deli=1&RQT=309&Dtp=1.

Gable, R., & Manning, M. (1999, January). Interdisciplinary teaming: Solution to instructing heterogeneous groups of students. *The Clearing House, 72*(3), 182–185.

Gabriel, A. E. (1999). Brain-based learning: The scent of the trail. *Clearing House, 72*(5), 288.

Gagné, R. M. (1977). *The conditions of learning* (3rd ed.). New York: Holt, Rinehart, & Winston.

Garcia, J. (1995, November). Edison's opening act. *Executive Educator, 17*(11), 24–26.

Gardner, H., & Hatch, T. (1989). Multiple intelligences go to school. *Educational Researcher, 18*(8), 4–10.

Garlikov, R. (1999). The Socratic method: Teaching by asking instead of telling [Online]. Available: http://www.garlikov.com/Soc_Meth.html.

Goodman, K. S. (1969). Analysis of oral reading miscues: Applied psycholinguistics. *Reading Research Quarterly, 5,* 9–13.

Gorney, C. (1999, June 13). Teaching Johnny the appropriate way to flirt. *The New York Times Magazine*, p. 43.

Grace, C. (1992). The portfolio and its use: Developmentally appropriate assessment of young children. (ERIC Document Reproduction Service No. ED 351 150)

Grant J., Johnson, B., & Richardson, I. (1996). *The looping handbook: Teacher and student progressing together.* Petersborough, NH: Crystal Springs Books.

Griffiths, R. (1999). Internet for historians, history of the Internet [Online]. Available: http://www.let.leidenuniv.nl/history/ivh/INTERNET.HTM.

Gronlund, N. (1995). *How to write instructional objectives.* Upper Saddle River, NJ: Merrill/Prentice Hall.

Grossen, B., Coulter, G., & Ruggles, B. (2001). Reading recovery: An evaluation of benefits and costs [Online]. Available: http://www.uoregon.edu/~bgrossen/rr.htm.

Haber, R. N. (1970, May). How we remember what we see. *Scientific American, 222*(5), 104–112.

Hansen, W. B., & McNeal, R. B. (1997, April). How D.A.R.E. works: An examination of program effects on mediating variables. *Health Education and Behavior, 24*(2), 165–176.

Haynes, C. (2000). Finding common ground: Chapter 14 [Online]. Available: http://www.fac.org/publicat/cground/ch14_1.html.

Haynes, C. (2000, August). Frequently asked questions about Head Start [fact sheet]. Washington, DC: Head Start Bureau.

Health Occupations Students of America (1999). What is HOSA? [Online]. Available: http://www.hosa.org.

Hickman, P. (1996). John Watson [Online]. Available: http://www.muskingum.edu/~psychology/psycweb/history/watson.htm.

Hiebert, E. (1994). Reading recovery in the United States: What difference does it make to an age cohort? *Educational Researcher, 23*(9), 15–25.

Hilliard, A. (2000, September/October). Excellence in education versus high-stakes standardized testing. *Journal of Teacher Education, 54*(4), 293–304.

Hiskes, D. (2000). Explicit or implicit phonics: "Therein lies the rub." *The National Right to Read Foundation* [Online]. Available: http://www.nrrf.org/essay_Explicit_orImplicit_Phonics.html.

Holzberg, C. (1996, November/December). Class trips in cyberspace: No passport required. *Technology& Learning, 17*(3), 58–65.

Horowitz, R. (1995, November/December). A 75-year legacy on assessment: Reflections from an interview with Ralph W. Tyler. *Journal of Educational Research, 89*(2), 68–75.

Horowitz, K. (1997). Focus on team teaching [Online]. Available: http://www.lalck12.ca.us/uc/asp/csp-ucla/past_articles/team_teaching.htm.

Hunter, B. T. (1998, November). Revamping school meal programs. *Consumers Research Magazine, 8*(11), 24–26.

Hunter, M. (1994). *Mastery teaching.* Thousand Oaks, CA: Corwin.

Huston, T. (1993). Handling sexual harassment complaints. *NASB Employee Relations Quarterly, 1*(2), 6.

hydi Educational New Media Center (1999). Inquiry learning [Online]. Available: http://www.wnp.ac.nz/onlinec/introcer/alpha/gym.htm.

Inger, M. (1991). Improving urban education with magnet schools. *ERIC Clearinghouse on Urban Education.* (ERIC Digests 76, No. ED 340 813)

Innovative Learning Concepts (1999). The TouchMath story [Online]. Available: http://www.touchmath.com/intro/touchmathstory.html.

Institute for Learning Sciences (1994). What the experts say about memorization [Online]. Available: http://www.ils.nwu.edu/~e_for_e/nodes/NODE-364-pg.htm.

Janofsky, M. (2000, September 16). Antidrug program's end stirs up Salt Lake City. *The New York Times,* A9.

Jensen, E. (2001). Brain-based learning: Truth or deception? [Online]. Available: http://jlcbrain.com/truth.html.

Jumpstart. (2000). About Jumpstart [Online]. Available: http://www.jstart.org/about/results.cfm

Kallio, B. R., & Sanders, E. T. (1999). An alternative school collaboration model. *American Secondary Education, 28*(2), 27–36.

Kearsley, G. (2001). Explorations in learning and instruction: The theory into practice database [Online]. Available: http://tip.psychology.org/bruner.html.

Kemerling, G. (1996). John Locke [Online]. Available: http://www.philosophypages.com/ph/lock.htm.

Kendall, J. S., & Marzano, R. J. (2000). Content knowledge: Compendium of standards and benchmarks for K–12 education. Monograph of the McREL Association for Supervision and Curriculum Development (3rd ed.), 673–682.

Kevin, K., & Krull, H. (1980). *Sometimes my mom drinks too much.* Milwaukee, WI: Raintree Children's Books.

Kohn, A. (1993). *Punished by rewards: The trouble with gold stars, incentive plans, A's, praise and other bribes.* Boston: Houghton Mifflin.

Kohn, A. (2000a, September). Standardized testing and its victims. *Education Week, 20*(4), 46–47.

Kohn, A. (2000b, December). High-stakes testing as educational ethnic cleansing. *The Education Digest, 66*(4), 13–18.

Kozol, J. I. (1985). *Illiterate America.* New York: Anchor Press/Doubleday & Company, Inc.

Kuskin, K. (1973). *What did you bring me*? New York: Harper & Row, Publishers.

Ladd, D. (2000). The Edison story: What's up with Edison [Online]. Available: http://shutup101.com/edison.

Landry, R. J. (1998, May). Bexar County D.A.R.E. program evaluation summary. In *A D.A.R.E. program survey in Bexar County, Texas.*

Lave, J., & Wenger, E. (1991). *Situated learning: Legitimate peripheral participation.* Cambridge, UK: Cambridge University Press.

Law, N. (1995, April). On the relevance of intelligence: Applications for classrooms? *Intelligence testing: The good, the bad, and the ugly.* (ERIC Document Reproduction Service No. ED 387 503)

Lepper, M. R. (1988). Motivational considerations in the study of instruction. *Cognition and Instruction, 5*(4), 289–309.

Levin, H. (1991, Winter). What are accelerated schools? *Accelerated Schools, 1*(1), 1–15.

Levine, D., & Levine, R. (1999). Two routes to unusual effectiveness: Dealing with doability and other correlates in the effective school process. *Phi Delta Kappan* [Online]. Available: http://www.pdkintl.org/prodev/nces/feature2s.htm.

Lezotte, L. W. (1995). Effective schools: Building foundations for school improvement. *The Video Journal of Education, 4*(8).

Library of Congress. (2000). Project on the "Decade of the Brain" [Online]. Available: http://lcweb.loc.gov/loc/brain/.

Lickona, T. (2000). What is character education? [Online]. Available: www.cortland.edu/www/c4n5rs/ce_iv.htm.

Lieber, J., Hanson, M., Beckman, P., & Odom, S. (2000, Fall). Key influences on the initiation and implementation of inclusive preschool. *Journal of Exceptional Children, 67,* 83–98.

Lindroth, L. (2000, September). How to choose educational portals. *Teaching PreK–8, 31*(1), 20–23.

Linguarama. (1999). Mind mapping [Online]. Available: http://www.linguarama.com/ps/196-2.htm.

Lonberger, R., & Lonberger, W. (1995). Enhancing literacy skills with a time capsule. *Teaching PreK–8, 25,* 52–53.

Long, Z. (1991, April). The effects of assertive discipline on children's attitudes toward school. (ERIC Document Reproduction Service No. ED 546 636.) Paper presented at the annual meeting of the American Educational Research Association, Boston, MA.

Lynam, D. R., Milich, R., Zimmerman, R., Novak, S. P., Logan, T. K., Martin, C., Leukefeld, C., & Clayton, R. (1999). Project D.A.R.E.: No effects at 10-year follow-up. *Journal of Consulting and Clinical Psychology, 67*(4), 590–593.

Mager, R. (1975). *Preparing objectives for instruction* (2nd ed.). Belmont, CA: Fearon.

Malawer, M. A. (1994). "My kid beat up your honor student." *Teacher Magazine, 6,* 40–41.

Martinez, C. R., & Lopez, J. R. (1999). "Stop, think and listen to the heart": Literature discussion in a primary bilingual classroom. *New Advocate, 12*(14), 377–379.

Maslow, A. (1970). *Motivation and personality.* New York: Harper & Row.

Mason, J. (1980). When do children begin to read: An exploration of four-year-old children's letter and word reading competencies. *Reading Research Quarterly, 15,* 203–225.

Mathis, D. (1996). *The effect of the Accelerated Reader program on reading comprehension.* New York: Random House.

Mayer, R. E. (1983). Can you repeat that: Qualitative effects of repetition and advance organizers on learning from science prose. *Journal of Educational Psychology, 75,* 40–49.

Meador, G. (1993). Thoughts on Hunter's Mastery Teaching Model [Online]. Available: http://www.ourworld.compuserve.com/homepages/meadorman/hunter.html.

Miles, S. (1997, September 12). Wired schools tackle Net pitfalls. In CNET News.com [Online]. Available: http://news.cnet.com/news/0-1005-200-322081.html.

Mindmap (1999). Mind mapping FAQ [Online]. Available: http://www/world.std.com/~emagic/mindmap.html.

Modern Red Schoolhouse. (2000). About Modern Red Schoolhouse [Online]. Available: http://www.mrsh.org.

Morgan, H. (1992). *An analysis of Gardner's theory of multiple intelligence.* Presented at the Annual Meeting of the Eastern Educational Research Association, Georgia.

Moshman, D. (1982). Exogenous, endogenous, and dialectical constructivism. *Developmental Review, 2,* 371–384.

National Education Association and American Federation of Teachers (1998–1999). School vouchers: The emerging track record [Online]. Available: http://www.weac.org/Resource/1998-99/april99/vouch track.htm.

National Council of Teachers of Mathematics (1998). *Curriculum and evaluation standards for school mathematics.* Reston, VA: National Council of Teachers of Mathematics.

Neuman, S. (2000). How can we enable all children to achieve? *Scholastic Early Childhood Today, 15*(1), 21–24.

Neumayr, J. (2000). *The Socratic method* [Online]. Available: http://www.thomasaquinas.edu/curriculum/socratic.htm.

New York University School of Law (2001). Jerome Bruner [Online]. Available: http://www.law.nyu.edu/faculty/bios/brunerj.html.

Nichols, J., & Utesch, W. (1998). An alternative learning program: Effects on student motivation and self-esteem. *Journal of Educational Research, 91*(5), 272–278.

Northwest Regional Educational Laboratory (2001). Catalog of school reform models: Montessori (Pre-K–8) [Online]. Available: http:www.nwrel.org/scpd/natspec/catalog/montessori.htm.

Office of Education Research (1993). Success for all. *Consumer Guide, 5,* 5.

Office of the Press Secretary (2000). [Online]. Available: www.state. gov.press.

Office of Special Education Programs (1995). Seventeenth annual report to Congress, Chapter 1: Students with disabilities served, placement and exiting patterns, and personnel who provide special education and related services [Online]. Available: http://www.ed.gov/pubs/ OSEP95AnlRpt/execsum.html.

Olaf, M. (2001). Products from "Child of the World," Michael Olaf's Essential Montessori [Online]. Available: http://www.michaelolaf.com.

Oldfather, P., & Dahl, K. (1995). Toward a social constructivist reconceptualization of intrinsic motivation for literacy learning. *National Reading Research Center, Perspectives in Reading Research, 6,* 1–19.

Orange, C. (1997). Gifted students and perfectionism. *Roeper Review, 20*(1), 39–41.

Orange, C. (1999, Fall). Using peer models to teach self-regulation. *Journal of Experimental Education, 68*(1), 21–31.

People for the American Way. (2001). What's wrong with school voucher proposals. Washington, DC [Online]. Available: http://www. pfaw.org/issues/education/voucher.criteria.html.

Perma-Bound Books. (2000). *Accelerated reader* [Online]. Available: http://www.perm-bound.com/arinfo.htm.

Perrone, V. (1991). On standardized testing [Online]. Available: http:// ereiceece.org/pubs/digests/1991/perron91.html.

Petch-Hogan, B., & Haggard, D. (1999, Spring). The inclusion debate continues. *Kappa Delta Phi Record, 35*(3), 128–131.

Peterson, H. (1996). Edwin R. Guthrie [Online]. Available: http://www. muskingum.edu/~psychology/psycweb/history/Guthrie.htm.

Pett, J. (1990). What is authentic evaluation? Common questions and answers. *Fair Test Examiner, 4,* 8–9.

Piaget, J. (1970). Piaget's theory. In P. Mussen (Ed.), *Handbook of child psychology* (3rd. ed., pp. 703–732). New York: Wiley.

Pinnell, G., Lyons, C., Deford, D., Bryk, A., & Seltzer, M. (1994). Comparing instructional models for the literacy education of high-risk first graders. *Reading Research Quarterly, 29*(1), 9–38.

Pipho, C. (1998). Living with zero tolerance. *Phi Delta Kappa, 79*(10), 725–726.

Poole, C. (1997). Maximizing learning: A conversation with Renate Nummela Caine. *Educational Leadership, 56*(6), 11–15.

Potter, L. (1997). Building reform around Adler's Paideia proposal. *American Secondary Education, 25,* 24–28.

Premack, D. (1965). Reinforcement theory. In D. Levine (Ed.), *Nebraska symposium on motivation: Vol. 13.* Lincoln: University of Nebraska Press.

Price, C., & Kuhn, B. (1996, May/August). Public and private efforts for the National School Lunch Program. *Children's Diets,* 51–57.

Price, J. H. (1999, August 8). Parents complain, "whole math doesn't add up on tests." *The Washington Times,* C9.

Raywid, M. (1990). Alternative education: The definition problem. *Changing Schools, 31.*

Raywid, M. (1994). Alternatives and marginal students. In M. Wang & M. Reynolds (Eds.), *Making a difference for students at risk: Trends and alternatives.* Thousand Oaks, CA: Corwin Press.

Raywid, M. (1998). The journey of the alternative schools movement: Where it's been and where it's going. *High School Magazine, 6*(2), 10–14.

Reddy, S. S., Utley, C. A., Delquadri, J. C., Mortweet, S. L., Greenwood, C. R., & Bowman, V. (1999). Peer tutoring for health and safety. *Teaching Exceptional Children, 31*(3), 44–52.

Reiff, J. (1992). *Learning styles.* Washington, DC: National Education Association.

Reinemeyer, E. (1996). Edward Lee Thorndike [Online]. Available: http://www.muskingum.edu/~psychology/psycweb/history/thorndike.htm.

Reith, H. J., & Ocala, C. (1984). An analysis of teacher activities and student outcomes in secondary school resource room programs for mildly handicapped students. (ERIC Document Reproduction Service No. ED 270 925)

Research Triangle Institute (1994, September). Past and future directions of the D.A.R.E. program. *American Journal of Public Health,* p. 1399.

Reyhner, J. (1998). *What's immersion education?* Presented at the 1998 Symposium of the National Foreign Language Center [Online]. Available: http://www.lll.hawaii.edu/web/haw/si98/deb/vocab.html

Ringwalt, C. R., Greene, J. M., Salt, S. T., Iachan, R., & Clayton, R. R. (1994). Past and future directions of the D.A.R.E. program: An evaluation review. Draft final report to National Institute of Justice. Research Triangle Park, NC: Research Triangle Institute.

Robinson, D. H., & Kiewra, K. A. (1995). Visual argument: Graphic organizers are superior to outlines in improving learning from text. *Journal of Educational Psychology, 87,* 455–467.

Rogers, C. (1969). *Freedom to learn.* Columbus, OH: Merrill.

Rose, T. (1999). Can charter schools meet the challenge? *Education Digest, 65*(2), 50–54.

Rotter, J. (1966). Generalized expectancies for internal versus external control of reinforcements. *Psychological Monographs, 80,* 1–28.

Scarborough Board of Education (1997). Policy on Assessment and Evaluation (p. 22).

Schamber, S. (1999). Surviving team teaching's good intentions. *Education Digest, 64*(8), 18–23.

Schmoke, K. (1999, August). Why school vouchers can help inner-city children. *Civic Bulletin 20,* 1–5 [Online]. Available: http://www.manhattan-institute.org/html/cb_20.htm.

Schnaiberg, L. (1997, March 12). Mother seeks honors status for daughter in special education classes. *Education Week, 16,* 13.

School of Teaching and Learning, The Ohio State University. (2000, September). Research, centers, & partnerships: Reading recovery [Online]. Available: http://www.coe.ohio-state.edu/edtl/rcp-readingrecovery.htm.

Schunk, D. (1991). *Learning theories: An educational perspective*. Englewood Cliffs, New Jersey: Prentice Hall.

Schunk, D. H. (1996). *Learning theories: An educational perspective*. Englewood Cliffs, NJ: Prentice Hall.

Schunk, D. (2000). *Learning theories*. Englewood Cliffs, NJ: Prentice Hall.

Scott, L. (1999). *The accelerated reader program, reading achievement, and attitude of students with learning disabilities*. New York: New York University Press.

Sensenbaugh, R. (1994). Effectiveness of Reading Recovery programs. *Reading Research and Instruction, 34*(1), 73–76.

Short, D. (1993, Winter). Assessing integrated language and content instruction. *TESOL Quarterly, 27*(4), 627–656.

Skinner, B. (1953). *Science and human behavior*. New York: Free Press.

Slavin, R. (1996). *Every child, every school: Success for all*. Newbury Park, CA: Corwin Press.

Slavin, R. (1997). *Educational psychology: Theory and practice* (5th ed.). Needham Heights, MA: Allyn & Bacon.

Soleil, G. (1999). Creating effective alternatives for disruptive students. *The Clearing House, 73*(2), 107–113.

Sousa, D. (1998). *How the brain learns*. Thousand Oaks, CA: Corwin Press.

Spearman, C. (1927). *The abilities of man: Their nature and measurement*. New York: Macmillan.

Stout, K. (1996). Special education inclusion [Online]. Available: http://www.weac.org/resource/june96/speced.htm.

Styfco, S., & Zigler, E. (2000). Pioneering steps (and fumbles) in developing a federal preschool intervention. *Topics in Early Childhood Special Education* [Online] 20, 67–70.

Sulzby, E., Barnhart, J., & Hiesima, J. (1990). *Forms of writing and rereading from writing: A preliminary report*. In Jana M. Mason (Ed.). Needham Heights, MA: Allyn & Bacon.

Sweeny, B. (1990). The new teacher mentoring process: A working model [Online]. Available: http://www.teachermentor.com/Mcentersite/MentoringProcess.html.

Sweet, D. (1986). *Extra-curricular activities participants outperform other students*. Washington, DC: Office of Educational Research and Improvement.

Tancredo, T. (1994). What's wrong with "outcome-based education"? [Online]. Available: http://i2i.org/SuptDocs/IssuPprs/IsOBEduc.htm.

Tannenbaum, J.-E. (2000). Practical ideas on alternative assessment for ESL students [Online]. Available: http://www.kidsource.com/kidsource/content2/practical.assessment.4.html.

Teale, W. (1986). The beginnings of reading and writing: Written language development during the preschool and kindergarten years. In M. Sampson (Ed.), *The pursuit of literacy: Early reading and writing*. Dubuque, IA: Kendall/Hunt Publishing Company.

Tella, S. (1996). The modern concept of man's knowledge and learning. In Seppo Tella (Ed.), *Two cultures coming together. Part 3. Theory and practice in communicative foreign language methodology* [Online]. Available: http://www.helsinki.fi/~tella/concept.html.

Terman, L. M., Baldwin, B. T., & Bronson, E. (1925). Mental and physical traits of a thousand gifted children. In L. M. Terman (Ed.), *Genetic studies of genius (Vol. 1).* Stanford, CA: Stanford University Press.

Thomas, R. (1992, Dec.). Reading recovery. *Education Consumer Guide* [Online], 3. Available: http://www.ed.gov/pubs/or/consumerguides/readrec.html.

Thurstone, L. L. (1938). Primary mental abilities. *Psychometric Monographs, 1.*

Tozer, S. (1998). *School and society.* Boston: McGraw-Hill.

Trailblazers (2001). A program with a purpose [Online]. Available: http://www.trailblazers.org.

Turner, S., Norman, E., & Zuny, S. (1995). Enhancing resiliency in girls and boys: A case for gender specific adolescent prevention programming. *Journal of Primary Prevention, 16,* 25–38.

U.S. Department of Justice. (1994, October). The D.A.R.E. program: A review of prevalence, user satisfaction, and effectiveness. *National Institute of Justice Update,* Washington, DC.

University of Idaho (1999). Emergent literacy [Online]. Available: http://www.ets.uidaho.edu/cdhd/emerlit/intro.htm.

Vollands, S., Topping, K., & Evans, H. (1996). Experimental evaluation on computer assisted self-assessment of reading comprehension: Effects on reading achievement and attitude. *Dundee Centre for Paired Learning,* 149. (ERIC Document Reproduction Service No. ED 408 567)

Vygotsky, L. (1987). *The collected works of L. S. Vygotsky* (Vol. 3). R. W. Reiber & E. A. S. Carton, Eds. New York: Plenum.

Warren, C. (1978). The magnet school boom: Implications for desegregation. (ERIC Document Reproduction Service No. ED 157 965; Clearinghouse No. UD 018 494, 1–5)

Watson, E. (1996). John B. Warson [Online]. Available: http://www.muskingum.edu/~psychology/psycweb/history/watson.htm.

Weaver, C. (1995). Facts on the nature of whole language education [Online]. Available: http://www.ncte.org/wlu/08894f6.htm.

Wertsch, J. V. (1991). *Voices of the mind: A sociocultural approach to mediated action.* Cambridge, MA: Harvard University Press.

Whitehurst, G. J. (1999). Research findings on emergent literacy and implications or family literacy programs [Online]. Available: http://www.whitehurst.sbs.sunysb.edu.

Williams, D. (1994). The layperson's guide to outcome-based education [Online]. Available: http://i2i.org/SuptDocs/IssuPprs/IsOBEduc.htm.

Wolf, D. P., LeMahieu, P. G., & Eresh, J. (1992, May). Good measure: Assessment as a tool for educational reform. *Educational Leadership, 49*(8), 8–13.

Wood, D., Bruner, J., & Ross, S. (1976). The role of tutoring in problem-solving. *British Journal of Psychology, 66,* 181–191.

Wozniak, R. H. (1996). Mind and body: Rene Descartes to William James [Online]. Available: http://serendip.brynmawr.edu/mind/Descartes.html.

Wronkovich, M. (2000, Summer). Will charter schools lead to a systemic reform of public education? *American Secondary Education, 28*(4), 3–8.

Zimmerman, B. J. (1989). Social cognitive view of self-regulated academic learning. *Journal of Educational Psychology, 81,* 329–339.

Zimmerman, B. J., & Martinez-Pons, M. (1990). Student differences in self-regulated learning: Relating grade, sex and giftedness to self-efficacy and strategy use. *Journal of Educational Psychology, 82,* 51–59.

Index

CORWIN
PRESS

The Corwin Press logo—a raven striding across an open book—
represents the happy union of courage and learning. We are a
professional-level publisher of books and journals for K–12
educators, and we are committed to creating and providing
resources that embody these qualities. Corwin's motto is
"Success for All Learners."